First published 2024

(c) 2024 Dominic Salles

All rights reserved. The right of Dominic Salles to be identified as the Author of this has been asserted by them in accordance with the Copyright, Designs and Patents Act 1988. No part of this work may be reproduced, stored in a retrieval system, transmitted in any form or by any means, electronic, mechanical, photocopying, recording, or otherwise, without the prior permission of the Author.

About the Author

Dominic Salles runs Mr Salles Teaches English, the YouTube channel where 22% of students went up 3 grades from their mocks, 21% achieved a grade 7, and 55% achieved grade 8 and 9. It has 132,000 subscribers, and over 5 million views a year.

He has been an English teacher for 30 years, which makes him both pretty old and incredibly wise. Seriously, it takes 10,000 hours to truly master something, and that normally takes about 10 years. You thought he was joking about the wisdom part? (No, I really do know my manure – yes it's just me writing this in the third person, because that's how these biographies go).

He still lives in Swindon, with his workaholic wife Deirdre. His jiu-jitsu-loving ex-engineer son, Harry, has moved to Shoreditch and lives on the site of Shakespeare's first theatre. Destiny. For those of you who remember Bob, he is now an ex-dog. It's curtains for him and The Curtain for Harry.

His daughter Jess has moved to New Zealand where the surf is higher, and the rugby is better than Wales. He spent three months in Andorra in 2022, learning to snowboard. He is not as cool as he thinks. In fact he is back in Andorra suffering from concussion.

His sister Jacey is an actress, famous for her Spanish accent, on your TV screens in shows like Casualty and Cold Feet. She would be hilarious in her own YouTube channel. Tweet her to let her know.

He drives a Toyota Prius and had solar panels fitted this year to offset his enormous carbon footprint.

Since you are still here, you might like to know that he grew up in Ibiza, his father gambled away two businesses and the family home, so 10 year old Mr Salles became an illegal immigrant in Canada, along with his mum and sister, before getting deported to the UK a year later, being homeless for 17 months, and receiving free school meals for the whole of his secondary school career. He went to 11 schools in total: 3 in London, 3 in Canada, and 5 in Ibiza.

He trained as a primary school teacher, packed it in because small kids infuriated him, and did an English degree, became a highly skilled tax inspector for four years, before taking a 50% salary cut to follow his wife into teaching, aged 28, and then refused any sort of promotion for 10 years so he could just learn how to teach.

He was happy in this life of poverty, became a strongman – yes, the lorry pulling kind – then a father, and put another 10,000 hours into being head of English, and then a further 10,000 into being a school leader.

Because he's had this sort of obsessive experience, his books, teaching and advice are generally pretty different from other teachers. Don't let that scare you. He doesn't see things that other teachers don't because he is crazy, it is just because he has been obsessing about it for soooo long.

It also convinces him that exams are damaging the study of English, that they encourage teachers to have very low expectations because what passes for a grade 7 these days is not hard and, truth be told, not very good. Even grade 9 is not that difficult, if you study hard.

So, his current obsession is showing average students the simplest way they can get top grades, and top students how they can quickly master the skills for grade 9 and beyond.

And, you know, maybe realise that English can be fun and a lifelong joy.

Other Grade 9 Guides by Mr Salles

Language

The Mr Salles Guide to **100% at AQA GCSE English Language**
The Mr Salles Guide to **Awesome Story Writing**
The Mr Salles Quick Guide to **Awesome Description**
The Mr Salles **Ultimate Guide to Description**
The Mr Salles Quick **Guide to Grammar, Punctuation and Spelling**
The Mr Salles **Ultimate Guide to Persuasive Writing**
The Mr Salles Guide to 100% in AQA GCSE **English Language Paper 1 Question 2**
The Mr Salles Guide to 100% in AQA GCSE **English Language Paper 1 Question 3**
The Mr Salles Guide to 100% in AQA GCSE **English Language Paper 1 Question 4**
The Mr Salles Guide to 100% in AQA GCSE **English Language Paper 1 Question 5**
The Mr Salles Guide to 100% in AQA GCSE **English Language Paper 2 Question 2**
The Mr Salles Guide to 100% in AQA GCSE **English Language Paper 2 Question 3**
The Mr Salles Guide to 100% in AQA GCSE **English Language Paper 2 Question 4**

Literature

The Mr Salles Guide to **GCSE English Literature**
Study Guide Mr Salles Analyses **Jekyll and Hyde**
The Mr Salles Ultimate Guide to **Macbeth**
The Mr Salles Guide to **An Inspector Calls**
The Mr Salles Ultimate Guide to **A Christmas Carol**
The Mr Salles Ultimate Guide to **Romeo and Juliet**
Mr Salles **Power and Conflict** Top Grade Essay Guide (AQA Anthology): 11 Grade 9 Exam Essays!

Books on Teaching

The Full English: How to be a brilliant English teacher
The Slightly Awesome Teacher: Using Edu-research to get brilliant results
The Unofficial Ofsted Survival Guide
Differentiate Your School: where every student learns more

Introduction

I don't have the copyright to publish these poems. But you can find them here at the time of writing.

Autumn by Alan Bold

http://www.holyfamilycarlton.org/wp-content/uploads/2020/03/English-KS4-Work-Lit-2-Unseen-Poetry-1.pdf

On Aging by Maya Angelou

https://allpoetry.com/poem/14326532-On-Aging-by-Maya-Angelou

The Richest Poor Man in the Valley by Lindsay Macrae

https://pmt.physicsandmathstutor.com/download/English-Literature/GCSE/Past-Papers/AQA/Paper-2/QP/June%202019%20QP.PDF

A London Thoroughfare. 2A.M by Amy Lowell

https://www.poetryfoundation.org/poems/53770/a-london-thoroughfare-2-am

Shoulders

https://poets.org/poem/shoulders

I Am Offering This Poem by Jimmy Santiago Baca

https://www.poetryfoundation.org/poems/53092/i-am-offering-this-poem

How the Guide Was Written

The quotes in the essays are made up from the poems. I have used synonyms, so that the sense is the same, but the language is different.

However, if the poet used a language technique, like alliteration, simile, metaphor, personification, contrast etc, the quote in the essay will use the same technique.

Every exam answer is taken directly from a student who has been marked by a senior examiner.

Again, I've changed the wording so that there is no copyright infringement. I've often got rid of words which the student didn't need and which scored nothing. So the answers are shorter. But they contain exactly the same points the student made, in exactly the same order, with the same range of vocabulary.

AQA's mission statement is **"Helping students and teachers to realise their potential."**

So, their answers should be freely available to all of us. They aren't. You can't get hold of them as a student, or a tutor, or a parent. You are not allowed to see them for free, and you are not allowed to pay for them either.

Only a teacher is allowed to give them to you. Many of your teachers won't know where they are – as typically only the head of department gets a link to that part of the website behind the paywall.

Home educated? In 2022, the DfE estimates that 116,000 students were home educated, a rise of 50%. All of them will eventually sit a GCSE English exam. Are they allowed to see exam answers marked by an examiner? No. They have to pay AQA to take their exam. But they aren't allowed to buy a marked answer.

Can you realise your potential if the exam board don't let you see what sort of answer gets each grade? Sure. But it won't be because AQA has helped you get there.

You will definitely get a higher exam grade if you do see answers at each grade, and so, that is my mission.

Helping students and teachers get grades 7, 8 and 9, no matter what their starting points or circumstances.

Although AQA are obviously failing in their mission, they are doing this for what they believe are moral reasons. They believe that giving out answers to past questions will mean that students can copy them and use them in their mock exams.

They believe this will undermine the integrity of the assessment system.

I'll let you judge that for what it is worth.

1. I am going to give 29 graded answers from grade 4 to grade 9.

2. You will see why the examiner gave it their mark.

3. You will understand what I think you should learn from each answer, and how to force the examiner to give you higher marks.

I would like to take this opportunity to thank AQA for creating a market for my work. AQA, you are letting your students down. Thank you for allowing me to help them to get top grades, because you don't want to.

The Mr Salles Technique

If you have watched my videos, you'll know I use the same technique for the unseen poem as for the poems in the anthology.

This has the mnemonic FOSSE Way.

F stands for Form and Structure.

O stands for the Opening.

S stands for SOAPAIMS – which is another mnemonic for **techniques**.

S stands for SOAPAIMS – which is another mnemonic for **techniques**.

E stands for ending.

Looking at it on the page now, FOTTE makes more sense!

So **FOTTE** it is.

Form and Structure

These are the most difficult things to write about, which is why both FORM and STRUCTURE appear in Level 6.

For Level 5, you need only *one* of these (according to the mark scheme).

Level 4 does not require either FORM or STRUCTURE.

So, if you write about these, the examiner wants to put your answer at least in Level 5, so grade 7 or 8! It's worth learning this skill then. (However, as you will see later, the examiner doesn't care if you don't have this skill – or so they say!)

Types of Form

The examiners are highly unlikely to give you a poem with a clearly defined form, like a ballad, or a sonnet.

But the poem will always be one of these two: free FORM verse, or RHYMING verse.

Free Form Verse

Free FORM verse is 'free' of RHYME. It is free from the traditions of the past, where poems always RHYMED.

So, free FORM always shows a desire for freedom, and to escape from control.

It often creates a sense of unease – we are not sure what to expect – in contrast to a RHYME scheme which, in poems written before 1919, always had a predictable RHYME scheme.

Free FORM poems always use ENJAMBMENT, because they always want to surprise. Enjambment always makes you think one thing, and then changes your expectation in the next line.

What you should write

1. Through FREE VERSE, the poet creates a sense of freedom and escape …

2. The poet uses FREE VERSE to show that society's rules don't always protect us …

3. The poet uses FREE VERSE to reveal how life is unpredictable, and we are consequently vulnerable …

One of these will always fit *any* FREE VERSE poem you are given.

Rhyming Verse

Pre 1919 poems always had RHYME schemes. This meant that poems had to RHYME in predictable ways. Everyone knew the rules. AABB? Sure, this poem is going to be written in RHYMING COUPLETS. ABAB? No problem, I can be confident that the next STANZA will follow the same pattern, CDCD.

Poets were free to choose lots of different RHYME schemes, but they had to be predictable and repeated within the poem.

You are unlikely to be given a poem like that.

But you are likely to get a poem with some RHYME in it. Rhyme is always about TONE. TONE is a technique which always puts your answer in at least Level 5 (grades 7 and 8).

What you should write about RHYME (and TONE)

1. The RHYMING COUPLETS create a humorous TONE to the poet's message.

2. The predictability of the RHYME creates a reassuring TONE, and hints that the ending will be positive.

3. The predictability of the RHYME creates an oppressive TONE, hinting that there will be no escape from X by the end of the poem.

4. The unpredictability of the RHYME creates a carefree TONE, suggesting that X is positive.

5. The unpredictability of the RHYME creates a sense of unease (an uneasy TONE), suggesting that Y might be negative.

One of these will always fit any RHYMING verse you are given.

What the Examiners Say About Structure

They literally say this:

We don't care about enjambment, caesura, end stopped lines, stanzas, rhyming couplets or all the other terms which teachers are making you use. We think about structure like this: write about the beginning and the end. That's it.

We don't care about rhyme schemes. No one ever has anything interesting to say about them.

If you have something genuinely interesting and meaningful to write about structure, go ahead. But, we read thousands of these, and hardly anyone has anything meaningful to say, so…

So, according to the examiner, you can literally ignore everything I've told you about free verse and rhyme (even though it is pretty helpful in understanding poetry).

For the examiner, it is not important that you understand poetry at all. Rhythm, stresses, beats, rhyme, half rhyme, syllable patterns – that's all voodoo, secret and distasteful stuff which should be kept hidden away.

The examiners don't ever want you to understand how a poem works.

They don't want you to ever write a poem. That would just be weird. Who does that? There's no poetry writing option in the language exam, is there?

No, they just want you to be able to write about **words**.

1. Why did the poet choose these **words**?
2. What is the poet trying to tell us about "the human condition?

Opening
The first two lines of the poem **always** give you the poet's idea. 100% of the time. Never fails. That's what poems do.

To make life even easier for you, the exam question **always** tells you the poet's ideas. 100% of the time. Never fails. That's what examiners do.

So, you always write about the opening of the poem. Every time you write anything, you always link it back to the poet's ideas. You don't have to work out what they are, or guess. They are right there, in the question.

Techniques
Literally anything is a technique, as long as you name it.

Every descriptive technique you've ever been taught. Every persuasive technique you've ever been taught.

TONE, RHYME, FREE VERSE, RHYME scheme, couplets, everything you've ever been taught about poetry, that's a technique.

Just flipping well name it when you are looking at a quote.

If you can't remember what it is called, just call it IMAGERY. Imagery is a technique found in 100% of poems.

Every poem is SYMBOLIC. One of the IMAGES will be a symbol of something else. 100% of the time. Never fails. That's what poems do.

So, always mention **symbolism** as one of your techniques – you won't lose any marks if you don't, but you will instantly hit Level 5 for that part of your essay if you do. Instantly!

Techniques

Techniques appears twice because you need to write about at least 4 quotes. You *may* not have named a technique when writing about the beginning of the poem, and you *might* forget to write about a technique at the end of the poem.

To be clear, you want to write about techniques ***every time you quote.*** But, just in case you don't, you need to hunt for two quotes to write about from the rest of the poem. You *could* write about anything.

So, narrow it down, by finding a technique.

These are the techniques which *always* come up:

1. Metaphor
2. Simile
3. Personification
4. Alliteration
5. Sibilance
6. Repetition

3 out of those 6 are guaranteed!

Ending

The ending, usually the last two lines, always reveals the poet's final point of view. 100% of the time. Never fails. That's what poets do.

If you write about the change in the poet's view, your answer is always "thoughtful". That part of your answer will be at least level 5.

If you've argued your point well, it will be "convincing" or "conceptualised", and that part will be Level 6.

Most students can do this!

You just get to the last two lines and ask, what does the poet want me to think about ... whatever the idea (or theme) was named in the question.

You never have to work out what the ideas *might* be, because they are right there, in the question! They are literally spelled out for you.

If you can (and you really can), name the technique used in the last two lines. And, if you can't name the technique, remember you can – it is IMAGERY, or it is SYMBOLIC.

BECAUSE THAT'S WHAT ALL POEMS DO!

Ok, I'll take a breath. I'm calming down. It's just that 50% of all the students I have ever taught can do **all** of these things in the FOTTE way. 50% can all get at least grade 7.

But, when you look at the answers in this book, you'll see that only about 10% of students in England do it when they sit this exam. 40% panic. Or don't believe in themselves. Or just get plain lazy in the exam, and write too little.

You can do better than them!

This is what the marks mean as a percentage:

Grade 9   88%   =   21

Grade 8   79%   =   19

Grade 7   71%   =   17

Grade 6   61%   =   15

Grade 5   52%   =   12

Grade 4   43%   =   10

You only need just over 50% for a grade 5, and 60% for a grade 6.

Most students don't even get 60%. But you will smash it.

Unseen Poem: Past Paper Questions

June 2022

In 'Shoulders': How does the poet present the need to protect and look after others?

Nov 2021

In 'A London Thoroughfare. 2 A.M.' How does the poet present ideas about night time in the city?

Nov 2020

In 'I Am Offering this Poem': How does the poet present ideas about the nature of love?

June 2019

In 'The Richest Poor Man in the Valley': How does the poet present the need to live in happiness and contentment?

June 2017

In 'Autumn': How does the poet present ideas of how autumn affects us and the world?

You will read answers from each of these papers.

10 Marks (Grade 4)

Response 1

'Shoulders' presents the importance of looking after people. **"Softly"** suggests the father is careful to make his son comfortable, just like checking the traffic **"twice"**. He protects his son from both the traffic and rain, allowing the boy to sleep. The rain *might* make it difficult for the father to check when it is safe to cross the road. **"No spray from a wheel"** shows that the father wants to stop his son from getting wet and cold.

The father *might* get to where he is going more quickly when he carries his sleeping son on his shoulder. This shows he is taking good care of his son. **"Precious goods"** shows that he loves his child. He loves to hold him close to protect him, and will put in a lot of effort to keep him safe from traffic and rain.

The poet suggests that even small actions are full of meaning. Love will help us all, as we all have difficult things to deal with. We should all look out for each other, every day in every weather. We must look after each other, as we are all vulnerable, and we need to be appreciated, just like this poem celebrates togetherness. We all need somebody for support, and that is Naomi's message.

She also wants us to look after the world as well as the people in it. We must protect it, because we live here, and must protect the air. We must protect the world and its people from pollution.

252 words

Original 346 words

10 marks

Examiner

- Paragraph 1 interprets the poem literally.
- It focuses on the word "softly", and looks at some details from the poem.
- Each detail has a relevant comment explaining a literal meaning.
- Paragraphs 2 and 3 show some understanding of the poem's ideas.
- It makes several comments to explain these ideas.
- These two paragraphs move the poem into Level 3.
- To get a higher mark in Level 3, the student needs to write about the poet's techniques.

Mr Salles Checklist of Essay Skills	
Thesis statement with one simple explanation	N
Thesis statement with two or more parts.	N
Form	N
Structure	N
Quotes from the beginning	Y
Quotes from the middle	Y
Quotes from the end	N
Number of one word quotes analysed	1
Number of quotes whether analysed or not	4
Number of techniques	0
Number of exploratory words	2
Connectives to suggest alternative interpretation	0
Conclusion	Y

Mr Salles

This is a student who clearly understands the poet's ideas brilliantly.

They just have rubbish essay writing skills – they don't name any techniques, and they use hardly any quotations.

Any comment on form and structure gets you higher marks, but this student didn't even *try* to do that.

This is an intelligent student who has paid no attention to how to actually earn marks.

12 marks (Grade 5)

Response 2

The effect of the season is shown with a comic TONE, **"Autumn sneaks in like a pick pocket"**. This suggests Autumn is like a man sneaking about picking leaves from the trees. He adds, **"with numberless painted baubles"**. This reminds us of the sense of awe we have from the colours of autumn and this stops us remembering that **"winter's snows will fall"**.

"The pick pocket steals warmth" shows that the picker of leaves steals our sense of joy and comfort. He also shows this by describing the sky which **"Rages with reddening cheeks"**. This too suggests that comfort and joy are being stolen.

104 words

Original 144 words

12 marks

Examiner

- The answer focuses on the words of the question.
- It deals with several techniques.
- It uses specific references and quotes.
- The explanations are relevant and make sense.
- The explanations of what the poet means *might* have been better.
- But, everything in the answer is relevant to each part of the question.

Mr Salles Checklist of Essay Skills	
Thesis statement with one simple explanation	N
Thesis statement with two or more parts.	N
Form	N
Structure	N
Quotes from the beginning	Y
Quotes from the middle	Y
Quotes from the end	Y
Number of one word quotes analysed	0
Number of quotes whether analysed or not	5
Number of techniques	1
Number of exploratory words	0
Connectives to suggest alternative interpretation	0
Conclusion	N

Mr Salles

This is another intelligent student. They understand the poet's ideas.

They also realise they need a range of quotes from beginning, middle, and end.

But again, there is no mention of structure – they don't even tell us which quote comes from the beginning, and which from the end. A waste of their talent.

You can see the impact of writing about techniques – just one technique has helped increase the mark, and the student has scored 50% with only 144 words. Imagine if they wrote 300!

Response 3

Angelou describes getting older as a drawn out experience. She COMAPRES herself to a forgotten book, **"Watch me silently sat, like a forgotten book in a bookcase"**. This SIMILE suggests she is abandoned and hidden from view. This portrays old age negatively. Angelou *might* imply that you lose self-respect and self-worth. Angelou tells us to **"wait"**, **"Stop! Hold your tears!"** The EXCLAMATION MARKS reveal that she rejects our pity, because *perhaps* she is accepting death.

Angelou also describes the lonely experiences of ageing, as **"I'll go on alone"**. This reveals that she prefers to face death alone, without help from anyone. The poem is STRUCTURED as a narrative. The poet starts speaking from her seat, and then ends with a sense that the poet is shocked, **"my breath still comes"**. This sounds as though she is saying **"farewell"**.

Angelou also describes the pains of aging, **"know my back is bent and breaking"**, **"Now you watch me shuffling, wobbling"**. Using the present tense **"know"** and **"now"** shows how old age is certain. Things **"breaking"** and **"shuffling"** is a negative description. This *might* frighten us about aging.

In conclusion, Angelou presents aging as inevitable, but you can't be certain when it will start.

201 words

Original 238 words

12 marks

Examiner

- This is a clear explanation of the poem
- Every explanation is relevant to the question
- There are a range of explanations
- They are all backed up with references or quotations
- The first paragraph includes some techniques the poet uses
- And the techniques are explained
- The student would get a higher mark if they added further detail to explain their ideas.

Mr Salles Checklist of Essay Skills	
Thesis statement with one simple explanation	Y
Thesis statement with two or more parts.	N
Form	Y
Structure	N
Quotes from the beginning	Y
Quotes from the middle	Y
Quotes from the end	Y
Number of one word quotes analysed	0
Number of quotes whether analysed or not	11
Number of techniques	4
Number of exploratory words	1
Connectives to suggest alternative interpretation	0
Conclusion	Y

Mr Salles

I love counting things. Numbers help me work out what has most importance.

This is an average student. I believe they are less intelligent than the previous two. This is because they have written very simply about the poet's ideas. In other words, they don't understand the poem as well.

However, they have scored 12, rather than 10, because they know what an essay looks like. They have most of the parts of the essay.

I'm hoping that, as we go through these essays, we will see a pattern which tells us the student is writing about the poet's ideas. These will be:

- Thesis with two or more parts
- An aspect of structure
- One word quote analysis

- Number of techniques
- Number of exploratory words
- Conclusion about the ending of the poem

And obviously everything linked to the poet's ideas. Come on!

This student mentioned it was a narrative structure, but this scored nothing. Why? Because they didn't then explain what the narrative structure tells us about the poet's ideas.

Response 4

The poet describes several ideas about the attitude to night-time in the city. The poem has a ridiculous STRUCTURE, with lines and paragraphs of varying lengths. This implies that random things can happen at night, so the STRUCTURE mirrors that.

Lowell begins the poem with a SIMILE to describe rain which is **"like a stroking hand"**. This reveals the speaker feels the night time city is calming and gentle.

Lowell describes the moon as **"her"**, PERSONIFYING it with **"her face is pale and pallid, she is my sister"**. This reveals that the speaker admires and loves the moon and what it *might* SYMBOLISE. It reveals that the speaker likes night-time in the city, as they stay awake to admire the moon.

The poem also REPEATS **"like a stoking hand"**. This implies that night *might* be tedious, but the speaker doesn't tell us one way or the other.

The ending of the poem is **"the city is a foreign country"**. This METAPHOR suggests that the speaker's love for it *might* be out of place, as though she doesn't belong there. It *might* suggest the speaker likes the city more at night than in day time, as they obviously stay up to see it when it is less hectic at night.

The speaker also thinks night time is beautiful in the city. The moon is described in a METAPHOR, **"her face, sharp and circular, slices the purpled sky"**. This is IMAGERY to create a picture in our mind. The word **"purpled"** reminds us of a bruise. This suggests the speaker feels that the city can stand up to the moon unlike the sky, and the speaker is therefore proud of the city.

280 words

Original 367 words

12 marks

Examiner

- The answer explains a range of feelings the speaker has about night-time in the city.
- The explanations are based on a range of quotations and references.
- The answer names three techniques, METAPHOR, REPETITION and PERSONIFICATION, which is a range.
- These are all linked to the speaker's feelings.
- To get a higher mark, the student should link these feelings to the poet's overall ideas.

Mr Salles Checklist of Essay Skills	
Thesis statement with one simple explanation	N
Thesis statement with two or more parts.	N
Form	0
Structure	1
Quotes from the beginning	N
Quotes from the middle	Y
Quotes from the end	Y
Number of one word quotes analysed	1
Number of quotes whether analysed or not	7
Number of techniques	7
Number of exploratory words	4
Connectives to suggest alternative interpretation	0
Conclusion	0

Mr Salles

Ok, there are loads of techniques, and lots of exploratory words.

But the examiner is saying, 'look, you've written very basic ideas that the poet might have. But none of them are developed. And some of them even contradict each other'.

What the examiner is too polite to say is that the student clearly doesn't understand the poem at all.

This is the least intelligent student so far.

So, why are they getting 12 marks if they have no idea what the poem is about? I mean, this is the beginning of Grade 5. How do they do it?

They aren't stupid. They work hard. They know the sorts of things that need to go into an essay, and they put in as many as they can. And they write as much as they can. 367 words.

This is my favourite student so far. They don't understand poetry, because they probably don't read. But they don't let that stop them working hard, and paying attention to what has to go in an essay.

Respect.

13 marks (Grade 5)

Response 5

Angelou shows the speaker's feelings about aging by focusing on one old character. She uses HUMOUR. Angelou COMAPRES them to a **"forgotten book"**, which is usually creased and hidden away. The character has **"a balding head and a shrinking chin"** and **"my back is bent and breaking"** This makes us sympathetic to the old, as their lives are more of a struggle. Instead Angelou orders us with the IMPERATIVES, **"wait"**, **"Stop! Hold your tears!"** She doesn't want people's **"tears"** or for them to feel sympathetic, because their **"breath still comes"**.

Angelou also points out the old person is still **"the youth within"**. She shows that we have a misleading view of the elderly because they are **"silently sat"**. The SIMILE **"like a forgotten book in a bookcase"** shows that people see them as forgotten.

Her use of COLLOQUIAL language, like **"jus'"** and **"cuss"** suggests that the old are still the same people they were when they were young.

The speaker views growing old positively, because they reject **"TV dinners"**. Angelou describes the old as **"blessed"** because their **"breath still comes"**.

179 words

Original 208 words

13 marks

Examiner

- Paragraph 1 is detailed, and focuses on techniques
- These techniques are linked to explanations
- The explanations are about the poet's ideas
- The answer shows how the techniques add to the meanings of the poem
- They use a range of quotations and references
- So this a clear response to the task overall
- The answer could be more detailed to gain a higher mark

Mr Salles Checklist of Essay Skills	
Thesis statement with one simple explanation	N
Thesis statement with two or more parts.	N
Form	N
Structure	N
Quotes from the beginning	Y
Quotes from the middle	Y
Quotes from the end	Y
Number of one word quotes analysed	3
Number of quotes whether analysed or not	14
Number of techniques	4
Number of exploratory words	0
Connectives to suggest alternative interpretation	0
Conclusion	N

Mr Salles

This is another smart student. But they frustrate me. They think about essays like this:

'I can understand poems. I must be good at English. But, because I enjoy the subject, and have no difficulty understanding what I'm taught, I'm cool. I'm not going to pay too much attention to what goes into an essay. I'll just quote a lot and write lots of explanations. I'll name as many techniques as I can. I'm happy with a grade 5.'

But, a thesis statement and a conclusion help you show the reader that you are building an argument. *That is what an essay is for!*

And, you know, it's a poem – poets are obsessed with the structure and from of their poem. Come on! All you have to do is say you are writing about the beginning and the end. It is that easy.

And 208 words. Does your hand hurt?

Please.

23

Response 6

Angelou portrays the speaker with a positive perspective on aging. For example **"Don't give me no TV dinners"** implies that the speaker doesn't need to lower their standards, as they are still **"the youth within"** as they were **"yesterday"**. Angelou portrays some old people as keen to pursue a full life rather than giving in to **"sloth"**.

Moreover, she portrays the speaker as appreciative of her luck, **"blessed am I that my breath comes in"**. The adjective **"blessed"** implies she feels lucky to be alive, even though she struggles with **"shuffling, wobbling"**, which emphasises her positivity about old age.

The poem's STRUCTURE also emphasises the poet's positive perspective. So the poem is a single STANZA, which *might* imply that we live only one life. Consequently, we must treat life as beautiful, be thankful for it, and enjoy each day as precious.

Angelou also uses REPETITION to highlight that the old can be strong, like the speaker, rather than weak. Consequently, she uses the IMPERATIVES **"Stop! Hold your tears! Wait! Hold your pity!"** to imply that the speaker needs no sympathy as she is coping well with being old.

188 words

Original 246 words

13 marks

Examiner

- Paragraph 1 is Level 3, until the final sentence which moves it into Level 4.
- This is the best part of the essay.
- It also uses a range of references and quotations to explain the poet's ideas clearly
- Paragraphs 2, 3 and 4 have only some relevant comments about the poet's techniques
- And only some awareness of ideas
- So the explanations about how the techniques link to the poet's ideas are not developed or precise enough
- Developing them and making them more precise would lead to a higher mark

Mr Salles Checklist of Essay Skills	
Thesis statement with one simple explanation	Y
Thesis statement with two or more parts.	N
Form	N
Structure	Y
Quotes from the beginning	Y
Quotes from the middle	Y
Quotes from the end	Y
Number of one word quotes analysed	1
Number of quotes whether analysed or not	8
Number of techniques	4
Number of exploratory words	1
Connectives to suggest alternative interpretation	0
Conclusion	N

Mr Salles

Most students write rubbish about structure. The poet chose a single stanza because they are unmarried, because the speaker is on her own, because they want to emphasise a single message, because they are pointing out we are all mostly interested in ourselves, rather than other people, because one is their favourite number, because they can't count up to two, because they didn't want to waste paper … yes, any of these could be true. But, you know this, they are all rubbish.

In the real world, only paragraph 4 says anything plausible about techniques. But the examiner is just ticking a box. Structure dealt with, no matter how unconvincingly? Tick.

And pretty much everything I said about the previous student, I'd say again here. It's nice to see a thesis statement, which the student returns to at the end. But …

Response 7

Bold uses a SIMILE to portray the effect of autumn which is **"Autumn sneaks in like a pick pocket snatching green bills"**. This implies that Autumn turns the green of nature into darker shades. The phrase **"pick pocket"** suggests criminality, which portrays autumn as very bad. We can all relate to this IMAGE of "autumn" as being bad.

Furthermore, the poem begins with **"Autumn sneaks"** which implies that we can't stop it. The word **"sneaks"** reveals that it will arrive unnoticed, so it has already got beyond our defences like a thief. This PERSONIFICATION implies that autumn will be with us for some time as we can't stop it.

Moreover, Bold titles the poem **"Autumn"** to emphasise that autumn is here to stay, and it is going to bring miserable weather. This reminds us to put on warm clothes, as autumn brings cold and wind every year.

The poem ends with PERSONIFICATION to highlight the climate and colours of autumn. The final lines **"the once soothing horizon rages with reddening cheeks"** shows how the world has become cold and dark. The word **"reddening"** implies that what was once light has become dark. The phrase **"reddening cheeks"** suggests anger which overcomes the warmth of summer.

204 words

Original 329 words

13 marks

Examiner

- This is mostly an explained response
- It identifies a range of techniques
- However, some Level 4 skills can be seen
- Especially the effective use of references and quotations.

Mr Salles Checklist of Essay Skills	
Thesis statement with one simple explanation	N
Thesis statement with two or more parts.	N
Form	N
Structure	Y
Quotes from the beginning	Y
Quotes from the middle	N
Quotes from the end	Y
Number of one word quotes analysed (inc. pick pocket as 1)	3
Number of quotes whether analysed or not	8
Number of techniques	3
Number of exploratory words	0
Connectives to suggest alternative interpretation	0
Conclusion	N

Mr Salles

Although the student hasn't mentioned structure by name, they have focused on naming the title, and naming how the poem ends. This is a subtle way of showing the examiner that you are dealing with the whole poem.

We could also argue that the title and choice of how to end are both techniques.

Writing about the ending also gives the examiner the feeling that this is concluding an argument, even though it isn't really.

14 marks (Grade 5)

Response 6

The poem deals with the idea of protection. We can see this in the language and STRUCTURE. Both father and son REPRESENT society, in order to convey the poet's message. The poem uses a speaker and another voice in this poem which is six STANZAS long.

The STRUCTURE emphasises the importance of protecting and caring for each person. The poem has a slow pace, because there are six STANZAS. This pace *might* SYMBOLISE the protective care the father has for his son.

It also implies that our society lacks care and compassion. This is reflected in the absence of a RHYME scheme. This *might* SYMBOLISE life's unpredictability. Because we never know what *might* happen, we are aware that everyone will need help at some point in their lives. This *could* make us reflect on our own lives and care for people in order to ensure a happier future.

This also CONTRASTS with negative aspects of society, which we will now see more clearly. Nye describes the boy with **"There are no labels warning breakable, precious goods"**. This *might* suggest that we are all unaware of a person's feelings or circumstances, because these things are hidden from sight. Therefore we should be kind and anticipate the suffering of others. This encourages the reader to change and *perhaps* seek to change others, in order to improve society for everyone's benefit.

In conclusion, Nye suggests that protecting others and being compassionate are the glue binding society together, and that without this it will fall apart.

252 words

Original 353 words

14 marks

Examiner

- Paragraph 1 shows clear understanding of the poet's ideas.
- This answer is particularly good at explaining the poet's ideas.
- Paragraphs 3 and 4 show a clear understanding of the purpose of the poem.
- To get a higher mark at the top of Level 4, the explanation of how the STRUCTURE of the poem links to the poet's ideas *could* have been made clearer.
- In addition, explaining other techniques would have led to a higher mark.

Mr Salles Checklist of Essay Skills	
Thesis statement with one simple explanation	N
Thesis statement with two or more parts.	N
Form	Y
Structure	Y
Quotes from the beginning	N
Quotes from the middle	Y
Quotes from the end	N
Number of one word quotes analysed	0
Number of quotes whether analysed or not	1
Number of techniques	8
Number of exploratory words	5
Connectives to suggest alternative interpretation	0
Conclusion	Y

Mr Salles

Ok, this is unexpected, isn't it? There is only one quotation! So, what is going on?

It tells us that the examiner is just interested *in the poet's ideas*.

Most of us will use quotations to reveal the poet's ideas, by showing what technique is being used in the quotation, and then showing how that affects the meaning of the poem.

This student has said, "ok, so actually, I can cut out the middle man – I can go straight to the techniques and use these to explain the poet's ideas. Also, if some of these techniques are about structure, I'm going to get a good mark."

Well, yes, you can do that. But it is harder to write about structure than a quotation. This is a very able student who has simply chosen to make life difficult. It is the equivalent of choosing to be a single parent. Worthwhile, but not as good as the alternative of choosing a partner to do it together.

The partner in this analogy is the normal, accepted parts of an essay. Just quote and explain. Write an argument which begins with a thesis statement. How hard can it be?

Please.

The structure comment about the 6 stanzas slowing the pace is complete rubbish. It might equally speed it up, or make no difference to pace at all!

The comment about not using rhyme is a comment on the chosen form. And as rhyme is always predictable, the students argument about unpredictability does make sense – it is not random. Hurrah.

Response 7

Angelou portrays the speaker with a negative view of aging. The speaker sees themselves as overlooked and irrelevant, **"like a forgotten book in a bookcase"**. This SIMILE suggests that the speaker fears being neglected as a result of growing old. A **"bookcase"** will also gather dust, which is like the speaker's feelings.

The first word of the poem, **"Know"** and the title **"On Aging"** shows that the speaker is already old, and already feels neglected. This *might* be a stereotypical view rather than the reality of old age. The use of EXCLAMATION MARKS and CAESURA in the fifth and sixth lines *could* REPRESENT the speaker's anger and frustration about aging. Conversely, this CAESURA *might* suggest the speakers lack of breath, which forces them to pause, because of their old age.

The command **"Wait! Hold your pity"** *might* suggest that the speaker wants to be seen as independent. This is emphasised by **"Don't give me no TV dinners"** and avoiding **"sloth"**. So the speaker refuses to give in to old age, and wants to overcome the difficulties of aging.

However, **"blessed am I that my breath comes in"** is the only positive view of aging offered by the speaker. This END STOPPED line emphasises that this is the only positive. The speaker manages to be grateful for life, even though **"my knees will fail the stairs"**. The expression **"so long"** *might* REPRESENT the death of the speaker, and *could* imply that old age leads quickly to dying.

246 words

Original 347 words

14 marks

Examiner

- The student is starting to explain ideas, which is level 3.
- However, the comments on the writer's techniques are Level 4 quality.
- It would get more marks if they wrote more about how they understand the poet's ideas.

Mr Salles Checklist of Essay Skills	
Thesis statement with one simple explanation	Y
Thesis statement with two or more parts.	N
Form	N
Structure	N
Quotes from the beginning	N
Quotes from the middle	Y
Quotes from the end	Y
Number of one word quotes analysed (Inc. So long)	3
Number of quotes whether analysed or not	10
Number of techniques	5
Number of exploratory words	5
Connectives to suggest alternative interpretation	1
Conclusion	N

Mr Salles

For Grade 5

My plan in designing this checklist was to show you how to write meaningful explanations about the poet's ideas.

1. You analyse quotes by referring to the technique used, and show how this helps explore the poet's idea. Using exploratory language and words like *however, although, in contrast*, helps you automatically look at alternative interpretations.

2. You link the ideas in a logical order, moving from beginning, to middle, to end of the poem. The end of the poem always deals with a new perspective – a fresh look at the poet's ideas.

3. The poet will also reveal their ideas through the choices they make in structure and whether to use rhyme (which you remember is our way of looking at form). So, looking at the structure and rhyme is necessary to fully explore the poet's ideas. I had thought this was going to be important, but you will see it is not important, even at grade 9!

4. Because an essay is an argument, showing your interpretation of the poet's ideas, it starts with a thesis statement, and ends with a conclusion.

For grade 5, you only have to do a bit of this!

1. Quote.
2. Write about the poet's ideas.
3. Write about techniques to explain these.

It's a very low bar.

15 marks (Grade 6)

Response 8

The speaker dislikes night-time in the city. She describes the city as **"dirty and dangerous"**, which suggest that it is harmful. She *might* fear the city at night because it is **"dangerous"**. Lowell also calls it **"a foreign country"** which implies how strange it is and suggests she dislikes it.

She uses SIMILES to reveal the speaker's opinions. It is **"like a stoking hand"**. This suggests that the city can feel gentle like rain. This links to the beginning of the poem **"They have smoothed the tarmac, it glistens in the street light"**. This suggests that the city can appear beautiful. *However*, the speaker feels this beauty is not real, and instead the city is **"like a stroking hand, Which becomes a fist"**. This implies that the poet has felt happy in the streets and then suddenly felt sad.

Despite hating most of the city, there is one aspect which the speaker enjoys: the moon. She describes the moon with **"her face is pale and pallid, she is my sister"**. This implies that the moon's beauty is comforting, and she says **"she is my sister"** which *might* compensate for how the city **"a foreign country"**. The use of PERSONIFICATION of the moon as **"her"**, and the expression **"I cherish her"** shows that she much prefers the moon to the city. It is only the moon which makes her feel calm and as though she belongs.

235 words

Original 302 words

15 marks

Examiner

- Paragraph 1 shows clear understanding of the speaker's opinions and feelings about the city at night.
- It uses relevant quotations and references to explain the speaker's attitudes.
- Paragraph 2 explains the effect of the IMAGERY.
- These comments would get higher marks if the student linked this better to explaining the speaker's attitudes.
- By the end of the essay, the student has shown understanding of the poet's ideas and the speaker's attitudes.
- They have also used references and quotations effectively.
- The AO2 comment on PERSONIFICATION isn't explained enough. Better explanation would have earned the top mark in Level 4.

Mr Salles Checklist of Essay Skills	
Thesis statement with one simple explanation	Y
Thesis statement with two or more parts.	N
Form	N
Structure	N
Quotes from the beginning	Y
Quotes from the middle	Y
Quotes from the end	Y
Number of one word quotes analysed	2
Number of quotes whether analysed or not	11
Number of techniques	2
Number of exploratory words	2
Connectives to suggest alternative interpretation	2
Conclusion	N

Mr Salles

One of the strengths of this answer is that it links ideas from different parts of the poem.

One way to do that is to say, 'this links'. Another is to introduce connectives like '*despite*' and '*however*' which automatically link to a different interpretation.

My top technique, for all grades, is just to write more.

The easiest way to do that is to use lots of quotes. Notice how the student links what they say about one quote to what they say about the next. It makes getting the marks very easy.

Despite being very good at English, the student still isn't writing an essay. If you don't write about the techniques, you are unlikely to write fully about the poet's ideas. Similarly, if you don't write a conclusion, you aren't properly dealing with the poet's ideas.

Response 9

The poet portrays the speaker's frustrated attitude to aging, as people view him as old instead of the person he once was. He feels stereotyped as alone and needing companionship.

The first line reveals his attitude, **"Watch me silently sat"**. This IMPERATIVE reveals the speaker's desire to change the reader's view of old people. It reveals how frustrated they are and makes the poem feel personal.

The speaker's attitude is also conveyed through REPETITION. The EXCLAMATION MARK in **"Wait! Hold!"** reveals how the speaker refuses to be seen as needing help, and rejects being viewed as a vulnerable member of society. This is emphasised through the REPETITION, and suggests the old should not be offered help until they request it. This reveals the speaker's anger and annoyance at being treated as different.

The speaker feels that growing old is inconvenient. The instruction **"Don't give me no TV dinners"** suggests the speaker doesn't want to be seen as stereotypically old, or as someone stuck in a chair who needs support. This rejection of **"TV dinners"** reveals that the speaker feels the old are treated as incapable, and also viewed as though they should remain inactive.

The speaker feels excluded and isolated as a result of old age. The instruction **"Don't get the wrong end of the stick"** implies that people don't value the old as members of society. Seeing them as full of **"sloth"** because he is **"exhausted"** is wrong, as they have benefitted society.

The speaker is attacking readers who *might* view the pension as an unnecessary expense for society. He points out the old have paid their taxes to fund this. So the poet portrays the speaker as accusing the reader, but also being thankful for being alive.

The final line **"blessed am I that my breath comes in"** gives an idea of the speaker's dialect. It gives them a distinctive voice. The word **"blessed"** shows how fortunate they feel to be living. But he is critical of government for their views on housing and pensions as a crisis. He views old people as a drain on taxes, even though they have contributed so fully to society.

In conclusion, the speaker is annoyed by society's attitudes to the old, believing them to be isolated and in need of care. Then he is frustrated that many people view the old negatively because the old stop working.

395 words

Original 664 words

15 marks

Examiner

- This answer is clear.
- The student understands the poet's and the speaker's ideas.
- They select some relevant quotes to back up their explanations of those ideas.
- There is only one part of the essay where they explain the poet's technique clearly, in paragraphs 2 and 3.
- So, they should write about more techniques, and link these to the ideas in the poem.
- (Notice how the examiner has ignored all the ideas which aren't relevant to the poem, such as government, taxes and pensions, and the lack of work done by the old.)

Mr Salles Checklist of Essay Skills	
Thesis statement with one simple explanation	N
Thesis statement with two or more parts.	Y
Form	N
Structure	Y
Quotes from the beginning	Y
Quotes from the middle	Y
Quotes from the end	y
Number of one word quotes analysed (Inc. TV dinners)	3
Number of quotes whether analysed or not	10
Number of techniques	3
Number of exploratory words	1
Connectives to suggest alternative interpretation	0
Conclusion	Y

Mr Salles

At last, a student who knows what an essay looks like.

'I'm going to write a thesis statement with at least 2 of the writer's ideas. I'm going to quote from the beginning, middle and end, with as many quotes as I can. Then I'll write a conclusion to summarise what I've proved.'

Not bad.

Notice this student wrote 664 words! Sheer effort got them a grade 6. Respect. If only their idea of what an essay looks like included explaining as many techniques as possible ***instead*** of as many quotations.

Writing about a technique will ***always*** involve quoting, unless you are writing about structure and form – so your grade jumps dramatically.

(Repetition can be seen as a technique of structure – so it is always worth looking for).

16 marks (Grade 6)

Response 10

Bold focuses on the unpredictable effects of autumn. The SIMILE **"Autumn sneaks in like a pick pocket snatching green bills"** reveals that change happens quickly, as though no one saw it. **"Green bills"** is an IMAGE of the leaves, when autumn changes their colour from **"green"** as they fall from their trees. The METAPHOR about the wind as **"his partner in crime"** shows how windy cold autumn is. The speaker portrays how the seasons bring changes which have an environmental impact.

Bold also uses PERSONIFICATION to show the effects of autumn leading to winter, **"winter's snows will fall from his fingers, smothering the face of the earth"**. The word **"smothering"** implies that the season is like a killer. Because this affects the **"face"** of the earth, it is as though nature is being killed. **"Snows"** implies that winter is worse than autumn, as it will freeze the world, so autumn prepares us for this change.

The STRUCTURE of the poem is a single STANZA, which *may* reflect how long-lasting autumn is, so much so that it feels everlasting.

178 words

Original 247 words

16 marks

Examiner

- This is clearly explained
- It shows good understanding of the poet's ideas
- There is a range of references and quotations
- These are used effectively in order to explain the poet's ideas
- The student identifies techniques
- And uses these to explain how these affect our understanding of the poet's ideas

Mr Salles Checklist of Essay Skills	
Thesis statement with one simple explanation	Y
Thesis statement with two or more parts.	N
Form	Y
Structure	Y
Quotes from the beginning	Y
Quotes from the middle	Y
Quotes from the end	Y
Number of one word quotes analysed	4
Number of quotes whether analysed or not	8
Number of techniques	5
Number of exploratory words	1
Connectives to suggest alternative interpretation	0
Conclusion	N

Mr Salles

This student is almost the opposite of the previous student: lazy.

'I know what an essay looks like, but I don't have time for that malarkey. And my hand hurts. I'm smart though, so:

- I'll just zap the examiner with a load of techniques.

- Stanza is the form of this poem, as there is only one – I'll smash that higher part of the mark scheme by writing about it, and I'll link it to structure.

- And I know they love analysis of one word quotes, so I'm all in on that too. Check it.'

So much potential wasted.

Response 11

The poem is concerned with what it means to live a full and happy life. The title JUXTAPOSES **"Richest"** and **"Poor"**. This suggests that financial wealth is not as valuable as mental health and positivity.

"His face and hands were lined by weather" marks him out as different to the rich, who will spend money on their appearance. **"His eyes were filled with sunlight"**. The verb **"filled"** implies that he is wealthy in happiness. He also provides happiness for others as his eyes provide **"sunlight"** to those who meet him. This **"sunlight"** is also an IMAGE of incredible warmth. This is a CONTRAST to the METAPHOR **"his face was furrowed by the wind and plough"**, and suggests his character CONTRASTS with his appearance.

At his funeral his friends are described as **"the congregation were baptised in their own tears"**. This METAPHOR illustrates how powerful his effect on them was. The word **"baptised"** implies that he has saved them somehow by being their friend. This is a huge CONTRAST to the impact of the rich, who seem to only acquire possessions. Even though he owned little. The word **"congregation"** suggests he positively affected many more people.

195 words

Original 262 words

16 marks

Examiner

- This is a very brief answer which manages to show all the skills of Level 4.
- It clearly understands the whole poem.
- It chooses relevant moments to focus on.
- These references are all used to write about the poet's ideas.
- AO2 is explained by focusing on two named techniques.
- These are well selected to explain the poet's ideas.
- To improve, the student should develop some of their ideas in more detail.

Mr Salles Checklist of Essay Skills	
Thesis statement with one simple explanation	Y
Thesis statement with two or more parts.	N
Form	N
Structure	Y
Quotes from the beginning	Y
Quotes from the middle	Y
Quotes from the end	Y
Number of one word quotes analysed	4
Number of quotes whether analysed or not	10
Number of techniques	6
Number of exploratory words	0
Connectives to suggest alternative interpretation	0
Conclusion	N

Mr Salles

Techniques make the mark!

Especially if the techniques include the poem's structure. Contrast and juxtaposition are *always* to do with structure.

Everything I said about the previous student is the same here.

You'll also notice that this student uses a more fluent vocabulary. They have a great understanding of how poems work, and understand this one very well. They are whip smart. Too dumb to put in the effort to get a top grade though.

Response 12

Bold portrays autumn as a "pick pocket" and a cause of negativity. This is achieved with an extended METAPHOR, which portrays autumn as a criminal. At the beginning, autumn is described in a SIMILE, **"like a pick pocket snatching green bills"** which is a negative portrayal of the season. A **"pick pocket"** is a criminal, which is a negative portrayal of autumn.

Later the METAPHOR extends to winter **"smothering the face of the earth"**. This METAPHOR shows the destructive change brought about by the cold. This clearly makes the poet feel unhappy. *Perhaps* the poet feels autumn and winter are negative as they steal away nature's colour and warmth.

These negative effects are also shown through PERSONIFICATION. At the end of the poem the narrator says that the sun **"Glows red with a quiet rage"**. The poem ends with a description of the sun when the **"horizon rages with reddening cheeks"**. The colour of autumn is the colour of anger. This PATHETIC FALLACY also reveals the poet's feelings of hatred toward autumn. We therefore understand his negative reaction to the weather and the season.

184 words

Original 274 words

16 marks

Examiner

- This is a clear, explained essay.
- Though short, it is clearly focused on the question.
- References and quotations are used effectively to explain the poet's ideas.
- The student identifies a range of techniques.
- These techniques are always used to explain the poet's ideas.
- So this shows an understanding of the whole poem.

Mr Salles Checklist of Essay Skills	
Thesis statement with one simple explanation	Y
Thesis statement with two or more parts.	N
Form	N
Structure	N
Quotes from the beginning	Y
Quotes from the middle	Y
Quotes from the end	Y
Number of one word quotes analysed (Inc. pick pocket)	1
Number of quotes whether analysed or not	5
Number of techniques	5
Number of exploratory words	1
Connectives to suggest alternative interpretation	0
Conclusion	N

Mr Salles

What is it with these grade 6 students?

They're all so damn lazy. They would stroll a grade 7. But no. They just want to splash out a few techniques, show off their vocabulary, their skills at writing quick explanations and, you know, finishing early, because that will look so cool in the exam hall. Nobody wants to be the one still writing at the end.

I do!

Response 13

The speaker offers happy experiences, love and kindness. The speaker keeps repeating **"it is you I love"**, which highlights how real and genuine this feeling of love is. The speaker also REPEATS the word **"offer"**: **"what else have I to offer?"** This *may* imply that the speaker is selfless, and so the love is genuine.

However, this love is also similar to that of a generous and kind parent, which we see when he offers to **"wrap you in safety"**. A further reference to suggest this is **"a jug filled with golden cream"**, whose IMAGERY suggests warmth. This is echoed by **"like a fisherman's sweater, the wind can't slice into"**, which is another IMAGE of warmth. This implies the speaker is addressing a child with a parent-like love.

In addition, the question **"and surely this is enough?"** reveals that the speaker believes they are offering the necessities of life, like kindness, to their child. This parental relationship also fits with the REPETITION of **"it is you I love"**.

In conclusion, we understand that this parental love creates safety and warmth, and offers life's necessities like clothing, a home and nourishment. This is typical of parental love.

196 words

Original 277 words

16 marks

Examiner

- Paragraph 2 reveals the student's understanding of the meaning of the poem and the poet's ideas.
- It uses a range of references and quotations.
- These help to support the student's explanations.
- The comments about IMAGERY identify techniques.
- The techniques are linked to the meaning of the poem, so the student shows a clear understanding.
- The range of explanations suggest that the student understands the whole poem.
- Even though this is a brief essay, it scores well because it is always focused on explaining the poet's ideas.
- They use references from the whole poem to show their understanding of the whole poem.
- To move to Level 5 they should add further explanation about the techniques and how these help us understand the poet's ideas.

Mr Salles Checklist of Essay Skills	
Thesis statement with one simple explanation	N
Thesis statement with two or more parts.	N
Form	N
Structure	Y
Quotes from the beginning	Y
Quotes from the middle	Y
Quotes from the end	Y
Number of one word quotes analysed	1
Number of quotes whether analysed or not	8
Number of techniques	4
Number of exploratory words	1
Connectives to suggest alternative interpretation	1
Conclusion	Y

Mr Salles

Lots of quotes, lots of techniques, relate everything to the poet's purpose, and it is difficult to fail.

This student also knows to include repetition as a technique as that fits the criteria of structure. The alternative interpretation always impresses the examiner as it is a real analysis of the poet's ideas.

But come on grade 6 people, write faster; write more.

Response 14

The speaker is afraid of the barren nature of the city at night, and their language is reminiscent of a prison. The STRUCTURE of the poem emphasises this fear, especially of the unknown. The speaker feels suffocated by the city. The SEMANTIC FIELD of **"caged"**, **"blankly"** and **"dangerous"** have connotations of being incarcerated by the city which surrounds the speaker. The word **"caged"** implies that they feel locked up inside this city without hope of escape. The adverb **"blankly"** and the adjective **"dangerous"** shows how lethal the city *might* be. The combined effect of this SEMANTIC FIELD is to highlight the speaker's sense of fear.

The speaker is also frightened at what is hidden, not just of the parts of the city she can see. Consequently the STRUCTURE of the poem appears disjointed. The moon is familiar, like a **"sister"**. This CONTRASTS with the city and its disjointed and unfamiliar nature.

The poem is a DRAMATIC MONOLOGUE, with irregular STANZAS and no RHYME scheme, which suggests a lack of control. This is designed to make the reader feel uneasy. This haphazard STRUCTURE deliberately CONTRASTS with the speaker's love of the moon, who is **"my sister"**.

So we can conclude that it is the unpredictable nature of the city at night which causes the speaker's fear. The FORM of the poem as DRAMATIC MONOLOGUE helps us understand the speaker's emotions, so that we too share this sense of fear.

238 words

Original 319 words

16 marks

Examiner

- Paragraph 1 shows a clear understanding of the speaker's attitudes.
- There are a range of references and quotations.
- These are all used to explain the poet's ideas.
- The answer names a variety of techniques.
- The techniques are all used to explain the speaker's attitudes.
- To improve, the student *could* write about one or more techniques in more detail.

Mr Salles Checklist of Essay Skills	
Thesis statement with one simple explanation	N
Thesis statement with two or more parts.	Y
Form	Y
Structure	Y
Quotes from the beginning	Y
Quotes from the middle	N
Quotes from the end	Y
Number of one word quotes analysed	7
Number of quotes whether analysed or not	8
Number of techniques	9
Number of exploratory words	1
Connectives to suggest alternative interpretation	0
Conclusion	Y

Mr Salles

Ok, it is short, but it is still what an essay should look like. It is a logical argument, from start to finish.

The original was just over 300 words, so about a page of A4, which is not lazy, though it is still slow.

There are a lot of techniques. The examiner's advice is most helpful here – explain more about the poet's ideas.

For Grade 6

Mr Salles Checklist of Essay Skills								
Response	8	9	10	11	12	13	14	Ave
Thesis statement with one simple explanation	N	N	Y	Y	Y	N	N	N/Y
Thesis statement with two or more parts.	Y	Y	N	N	N	N	Y	N/Y
Form	N	N	N	N	N	N	Y	N
Structure	Y	Y	Y	Y	N	Y	Y	Y
Quotes from the beginning	Y	Y	Y	Y	Y	Y	Y	Y
Quotes from the middle	Y	Y	Y	Y	Y	Y	N	Y
Quotes from the end	Y	Y	Y	Y	Y	Y	Y	Y
Number of one word quotes analysed	3	3	4	4	1	1	7	3
Number of quotes whether analysed or not	10	10	10	10	5	8	8	9
Number of techniques	3	3	6	6	5	4	9	6
Number of exploratory words	1	1	0	0	1	1	1	1
Connectives to suggest alternative interpretation	0	0	0	0	0	1	0	0
Conclusion	Y	Y	N	N	N	Y	Y	Y

So we can see that on average grade 6 students:

1. Have at least a one part thesis.
2. Write about structure – focusing on beginning, ending, repetition or contrast.
3. Use quotes from all parts of the poem – especially the beginning and ending.
4. Make sure they analyse 2 or 3 one word quotations.
5. Include 8 or 9 quotes.
6. Write about 4 – 6 techniques. They try to use these to write about the poet's ideas.
7. Write a conclusion.

In other words, they know what an essay looks like. They try to deliver on all the parts of an essay.

But they also tend to be students who could easily get a grade 7 if they weren't so damned lazy.

17 marks (Grade 7)

Response 15

Macrae portrays ideas about living a worthwhile and happy life through IMAGERY. She believes that happiness does not depend on materialistic wealth.

So the man is initially described focusing on his **"exterior"**. She says **"he appeared weaker than he was"**. This implies that his lifestyle has given him powerful knowledge and a hidden strength. She uses a METAPHOR, **"his face was furrowed by the wind and plough"**. At first glance, this is a negative perspective of his appearance. But Macrae follows it with **"His eyes were filled with sunlight"**. This suggests that he is filled with kindness and generosity, just as sunlight gives life to living things. This implies that he gives life to other people, through his generosity.

Macrae CONTRASTS this man to most people. He is happy, without needing **"wealth"**, **"a mansion"**, **"bank managers and other parasites"**. She uses ENJAMBMENT to highlight the word **"parasites"**. This implies that his happiness doesn't depend on the conventional things we associate with being happy. The poet describes how he was **"happy in a cabin"** until his death. This implies that he was happy even though he was isolated. It suggests that this is the most valuable form of contentment. *However*, she describes his friends at his funeral, **"the congregation were baptised in their own tears"** which suggests how much he was missed.

To conclude, the poet shows that a contented and happy life does not depend on other people, or material aspirations like **"wealth"** and **"mansions"**. This reveals that Macrae believes true happiness doesn't depend on the outside world.

258 words

Original 321 words

17 marks

Examiner

- This shows a clear understanding of the poet's ideas.
- The student uses a large range of references and quotations.
- The student keeps referring back to the poet's main idea with each reference to the poem.
- This is what we mean by writing in more detail about techniques. This student does it by looking at CONTRAST and alternative interpretations.
- To get a higher mark, the student should write about more techniques in this way.

Mr Salles Checklist of Essay Skills	
Thesis statement with one simple explanation	N
Thesis statement with two or more parts.	Y
Form	N
Structure	Y
Quotes from the beginning	Y
Quotes from the middle	Y
Quotes from the end	Y
Number of one word quotes analysed	3
Number of quotes whether analysed or not	12
Number of techniques	3
Number of exploratory words	0
Connectives to suggest alternative interpretation	1
Conclusion	Y

Mr Salles

Ok, we have developed ideas here. That just means:

- Writing more than one explanation about the same quotation.
- Or, finding more than one quote to link to the same explanation.
- Or writing about an alternative interpretation – here with 'however'.
- And writing a detailed conclusion with several of the poet's ideas in it.

Although there aren't that many techniques, 'enjambment' and 'contrast' are both about structure, which is at the top of the mark scheme: Level 5.

And the student was not too lazy – 321 words is ok!

Response 16

Nye presents the importance of protecting others and caring for them as a collective role in society.

The REPETITION of **"we"** emphasises that this is a collective duty, rather than just the role of the father in the poem. The REPETITION of **"will not"** which follows **"we"** implies that collective action is going to be difficult, and we will have to overcome our own desires to be selfish. **"We"** also invites the reader to join the speaker in improving society, *in contrast* to others who *might* not care about other people, or want to protect them.

Furthermore **"No spray from a wheel"** shows how the majority of drivers are selfish. The actions of drivers have a real impact on others. The poet wants us to agree on new rules for a new society in which everyone protects and supports others. **"No spray"** also emphasises that we must consider how our surroundings will affect others. *Perhaps* we *may* be driving with a team of work colleagues supporting each other, but we must still act together to support others.

The last line of the poem, **"The weather will never begin to care"** reveals that the natural world is already full of hardship and this also *may* work as PATHETIC FALLACY showing how other people don't care, so we must struggle to give everyone happiness. The phrase **"never begin"** reveals how hostile the world can be.

However, in the fourth STANZA, the boy is portrayed very positively, as he is protected from **"downpours"** and **"wheels"**. This is a further demonstration that our actions will affect others, so we must share joint responsibility for protecting and caring for others.

To conclude, these ideas of protection and care are a communal mission.

287 words

Original 419 marks

17 marks

Examiner

- Paragraph 1 begins by dealing with the poet's wider ideas.
- The student keeps coming back to these ideas each time they quote.
- This means that the essay is always going to get at least Level 5 for AO1 Task.
- The student treats the characters as constructs, to present Nye's ideas.
- The answer uses a range of references and quotes to explain the poet's techniques
- And the student explains how these techniques help the poet show their ideas.
- To get a higher mark in Level 5, the student *could* focus on one or more techniques with more detailed explanations.

Mr Salles Checklist of Essay Skills	
Thesis statement with one simple explanation	N
Thesis statement with two or more parts.	Y
Form	N
Structure	Y
Quotes from the beginning	Y
Quotes from the middle	Y
Quotes from the end	Y
Number of one word quotes analysed (Inc. 2 word quotes)	5
Number of quotes whether analysed or not	11
Number of techniques	4
Number of exploratory words	4
Connectives to suggest alternative interpretation	2
Conclusion	Y

Mr Salles

Is this our first essay with everything but form?

It's also our first essay where the student has put in a decent effort, writing as much as possible.

It's a bit light on techniques, which is what is holding this student back. More techniques would get grade 8.

Response 17

The poet illustrates the importance of each of us protecting one another. This will ensure the safety of the thing and people he loves. It will stop him feeling fear. We see this when the father is **"crossing softly, twice checking left and right"**. This immediately reveals how important his son is. It further implies that he is desperate to keep his son so safe, he even protects him from a splash of rain. The word **"softly"** emphasises the effort he puts into this care, and suggests he loves his son deeply. This REPRESENTS the need for us all to care for each other.

This urge to take care of others is portrayed as being the father's first thought. We see this as the father is described with **"he cradles the earth's most fragile treasure"**. This portrays his determination to keep his son safe. This also reveals that other people don't care that his son is asleep, so the father has to worry about the threat of those people. The quote also suggests that the son is breakable, and the word **"cradle"** shows how the father must protect him, no matter what cost. Calling him a **"treasure"** also suggests that he must keep his son safe as he is so valuable.

The poet REPEATS the idea of protection, **"There are no labels warning breakable, precious goods"**. This suggests the father has not learned how to protect his son, but is acting on instinct. It emphasises how he will try to keep his son safe and happy in every way possible. This reinforces the idea that we must all look after and protect others, as doing so will affect everyone's lives and futures. The use of CAPITALS also implies that protecting others is essential, just like the father emphasises the importance of protecting his sleeping son.

305 words

Original 461 words

17 marks

Examiner

- Paragraph 1 shows clear understanding of the father's feelings from the way the poet has presented them.
- The student uses relevant references and quotations to explain the father's feelings.
- The student explains the effects of an individual word, in this case "softly".
- The second paragraph also explains the effect of an individual words, "cradle" and "treasure".
- By the final paragraph, the student has a full explanation of the ideas of protection in the whole poem.
- To get a higher mark in Level 5, the student *could* write about how the poet's ideas about society are revealed in the poem.

Mr Salles Checklist of Essay Skills	
Thesis statement with one simple explanation	N
Thesis statement with two or more parts.	Y
Form	N
Structure	Y
Quotes from the beginning	Y
Quotes from the middle	Y
Quotes from the end	N
Number of one word quotes analysed	3
Number of quotes whether analysed or not	6
Number of techniques	3
Number of exploratory words	0
Connectives to suggest alternative interpretation	0
Conclusion	N

Mr Salles

The student writes about this theme of protection in a detailed thesis statement, and in the final paragraph, so the examiner has treated this as summing up the ideas of the whole poem. They have treated the final paragraph as a conclusion.

I haven't treated this as a conclusion. It is almost impossible to write a conclusion without writing about the ending. You can see that the last point the student was making was about capital letters – which happen half way through the poem.

My guess is that this is a student who simply ran out of time, and simply wrote the final paragraph by referring back to the idea in the thesis. This is smart.

It is even better if you have quicker hand-writing speed which, as you know, takes no brains at all.

Just practice.

I've also treated repetition as a reference to structure.

18 marks

Response 18

Nye presents the ideas of caring for others and protecting them as a natural and important parental instinct. The first STANZA portrays the father **"crossing softly … so his son still sleeps"**. The ideas of protection and care are suggested by the adverb **"softly"**. Moreover, **"crossing softly"** rules out any quick movement like running, which emphasises his level of care. The connective **"so"** emphasises that protecting his son is his duty, and the responsibility of every parent.

This is reinforced with the REPETITION of **"no"** in **"no spray"** and **"no wheel"** in the second STANZA. This shows that the instinct to protect a child is constant, and intense for every parent. These lines containing REPETITION are also END STOPPED. This *might* reflect the determination parents have in caring for and protecting their children.

In the third STANZA the son is described with a METAPHOR, as **"precious goods"**. His vulnerability is conveyed with the adjective **"precious"**, and reveals that we are instinctively drawn to protect and care for those who are vulnerable. Consequently, because we are all vulnerable at times, the poem suggests we all need to care for and protect each other. The poem implies that, like the father and his son, we cannot be safe unless we protect and care for each other.

The fifth STANZA implies that this care is a duty, otherwise we would not survive. The poem has a circular STRUCTURE, as it begins and ends with **"cradles"**. This *might* SYMBOLISE an outer shell, encasing the IMAGERY about care and protection in the middle of the poem. It shows that, when we look deep within, we must see that we all deserve to be cared for and protected. Because we are all vulnerable at different times in life, the ideas of protection and care are crucial.

300 words

Original 340 marks

18 marks

Examiner

- The essay is clearly answering the question.
- With plenty of detail and explanation.
- By the end of the essay, the student has given enough explanations to be judged 'developed'.
- All the explanations are about relevant details and quotations.
- Some techniques are named to explain the poet's ideas.
- The comment about the circular STRUCTURE is linked to the symbolism of the poem. This means that AO2 can be scored in Level 5.
- To get more marks within Level 5, the student should write about more techniques.

Mr Salles Checklist of Essay Skills	
Thesis statement with one simple explanation	N
Thesis statement with two or more parts.	Y
Form	N
Structure	Y
Quotes from the beginning	Y
Quotes from the middle	Y
Quotes from the end	N
Number of one word quotes analysed	3
Number of quotes whether analysed or not	10
Number of techniques	7
Number of exploratory words	0
Connectives to suggest alternative interpretation	0
Conclusion	Y

Mr Salles

This student believes that writing about structure is more important than writing about quotes. This is because it is in the marking criteria.

But, the marking criteria is misleading. The examiners' reports keep saying this:

Look, we just want you to write about the beginning and ending of the poem. This is plenty of structure.

We don't need you to say anything about end stopped lines, or caesura or enjambment. Also, when you do write about those things, you find it difficult to write about the poet's ideas.

But, when you write about the beginning and the ending, you will always be writing about why the poet starts and ends like this. So, you will always be linking the structure of the poem to the poet's ideas.

This is for real. Look up any Examiner's Report and find the 'Advice for Students' section. It is both practical and hilarious. I can sum it up like this:

*'We love you and your ideas. We don't actually need you to **know** anything at all about poetry. We just want you to be able to tell us what the poem makes you think and feel, and then link that to what it means to be human.*

Oh, by the way, we will tell you what it means to be human in the actual question! The Big Idea, the theme as we say in literature, is named in the question. Here it is 'protection'.

It will always deal with "the human condition". You are human, we are human, and that's why we love you, and we love literature.

This, sadly, is also for real.

All humans, for all of history and, we can be pretty sure, for all of future time, will always feel love, will always need to protect, and to be parents. To the examiner, this is "the human condition". There is no higher value, no greater topic, no more interesting idea to the examiner than "the human condition".

Every poetry question you ever get will always be about "the human condition".

It is a bit like saying all poems are made of words. True. So true. But profound?

In fact, while we are swimming in these warm and soothing waters, the examiners also believe every text you ever study – plays, novels, the whole raft of brilliance that your teachers float through the canyons of your education, navigating the rapids of the gothic, or of dystopian fiction, or the hero's journey, are all there to make you better humans, more aware of your desires and frailties, your despair and anger, your loves and hopes…

*Yeah, that's "the human condition". That's literature baby. Stop telling us what you **know**, and just tell us what you **feel** about the writer's ideas.*

…

So What?

Ok, I may personally believe that literature is about so much more than this.

But, relax. This guide is simply about how to get the grade in the exam.

So, you don't have to write about structure with any kind of specialist vocabulary. Just make sure that you write about the beginning and the end and show what has changed.

There will always be 'repetition' and 'contrast' in every poem. Write about those structural techniques. They are easy to link to the poet's ideas. So link them. Grade 7. Bish, bash, bosh.

The student has used the word STANZA correctly, and it is a structural feature of the poem. However, it earns no marks, as it does not link to anything about the poet's ideas. To be fair to the examiners, almost no one knows how to write about structure in a meaningful way.

It would be so much more honest and easier if the marking criteria said this:

Write about the poet's ideas from the beginning and ending of the poem.

Writing about the beginning and ending will actually help you understand the poem, the poet's ideas and what they want you to think and feel. It will also help you write a conclusion.

You can see that this advice would definitely have helped this student. Instead of writing about the ending, they have written about structure. But, in doing so the student used some magical words.

Circular Structure.

Yes, everything can be made to have a circular structure. Especially a poem. A poem will always have an idea at the end which is the same idea at the beginning, but presented in a slightly different way. ***All*** poems are made this way.

So, it is a bit like saying: 'this poem ends with words'.

But the examiner doesn't know this!

The examiner thinks that every poem ends in a different way. They think that only a gifted student will spot the hidden truth that sometimes, just occasionally, a poet pulls off the remarkable feat of ending a poem ***with a circular structure!***

So, that's a free grade 7 conclusion for you, every time.

Response 19

Baca portrays love as desirable, as a passion, and as a way to achieve power and to control. Reality is harsh, and the poem offers a moral purpose to help people cope with that harshness.

So the poem begins with a SIMILE, **"Wear it like a ski jacket when snow seeks to smother you or like snowboarder's mittens the winter cannot pierce"**. The violence of the IMAGERY, with the verbs **"smother"** and **"pierce"**, emphasises the harshness of nature. The objects of the comparison protect, but also conceal what is inside, *perhaps* the person's real nature. This emphasises that nature cannot be controlled, so we must try to protect ourselves.

This harsh reality is CONTRASTED with the dreamy TONE of the poem. The SIBILANCE of **"ski jacket when snow seeks to smother"** creates a sense of rhythm which is also found elsewhere in the poem. This rhythm *might* be used to reassure the reader. This links to the idea that **"winter cannot pierce"**, so the clothing is a great protection. <u>However</u>, *perhaps* this is a deliberate attempt to deceive the reader.

The repeated CAESURA of **"Take my love"** and the REPETITION of **"I"** and **"I own"** emphasise that literature and the poem is a powerful offering. It suggests that offering something should be enough, rather than expecting something in return. The TONE is also ominous. The poet emphasises **"I own nothing"** and **"this is all I own"**, which suggests that he is close to desperation. This CONTRASTS with the subject and idea of love, which makes us question the poet. The STRUCTURE of the poem, in four STANZAS, incorporating occasional RHYMING COUPLETS, feels consistent and reassuring, which SYMBOLISES the poet's love.

Baca's main purpose is to show that love can have a range of positive impacts on the emotions and mental states of others.

303 words

Original 403 words

18 marks

Examiner

- Paragraphs 1 and 2 show clear understanding of the poet's ideas.
- It is focused on the question.
- Paragraph 3 identifies a range of techniques.
- The techniques are used to explain the poet's ideas.
- The explanations use the right references and quotations.
- The penultimate paragraph has very effective and thoughtful interpretations of the poet's ideas.
- To get a higher mark in Level 5, the student should show the same level of interpretation about the poet's techniques.

Mr Salles Checklist of Essay Skills	
Thesis statement with one simple explanation	N
Thesis statement with two or more parts.	Y
Form	Y
Structure	Y
Quotes from the beginning	Y
Quotes from the middle	Y
Quotes from the end	N
Number of one word quotes analysed	4
Number of quotes whether analysed or not	10
Number of techniques	12
Number of exploratory words	3
Connectives to suggest alternative interpretation	1
Conclusion	Y

Mr Salles

This student knows stuff about poetry. They've understood that the structural choices affect the tone, and therefore the meaning of the poem.

The penultimate paragraph is actually a really convincing explanation of all the structural techniques it includes. This student is leagues ahead of the previous answer, the difference between going to Reading university or Oxford university.

But, the examiner is having none of it because they don't really care about the structure of the poem. They don't care that this is a poem and not a short story, or a novel, or a play. They don't care about the differences between these types of text.

'Just give me the human condition baby' – that's why they love paragraph 3.

Don't believe me? Well, there are 12 techniques! And the examiner says 'write about more techniques'!

This makes no sense until you subtract all the techniques which are about STRUCTURE. Caesura, rhyming couplets, stanza, structure … probably even repetition and contrast. That just leaves **tone**, **simile** and **sibilance** as the only techniques which the examiner really values.

But, it is at least useful to know this.

Write about the beginning and end of the poem, noticing any repetition and you've smashed the element of 'structure' from the mark scheme.

And, write a proper conclusion based upon the ending of the poem.

Response 20

The poet conveys their attitude to aging with a TRIPLET, **"Stop! Hold your tears! Wait!"** This IMPERATIVE instruction conveys a cold and abrupt TONE, showing how the speaker demands to be treated. The speaker doesn't want the help of others, which is indicated by the instruction not to release any tears of pity, **"Hold!" "Tears"** implies a feeling of pity that the old are vulnerable to being exploited. The speaker realises that the onlooker *might* feel that their attitude is caring, but the poet portrays it as patronising.

The speaker employs a sarcastic TONE, **"Do me this one thing:/ don't give me no TV dinners"**. The sarcasm is emphasised by the ENJAMBMENT. The use of **"do"** and **"don't"** is forceful and reflects the speaker's dominant personality. We are encouraged to think their view of care is warped. The kindness of others offends her, because she values her independence, and sees their care as robbing her of this.

The poet shows that age changes a person, both their bodies and their minds. She portrays the speaker as in denial about this: **"I am the youth within I was yesterday"**. This reveals the speaker's determination to remain in the past, rather than be treated differently because of her age. She wants others to treat her as an equal, rather than use their sympathy to treat her differently.

This is picked up in the description **"like a forgotten book in a bookcase"**, which reveals how the old are uncared for and abandoned. The word **"forgotten"** emphasises this. In addition, placing this book in a **"bookcase"** implies that all the old are forgotten in this way.

The instruction **"Wait! Hold your pity"** portrays the speaker as ungrateful at another's sympathy. Pity is a compassionate act, but the speaker dismisses it because of her warped perspective. She appears to think that pity will be followed by contempt and exploitation.

To conclude, the speaker believes aging doesn't lead to diminished abilities. She emphasises that the old are just as human as the rest of us, can remain independent, and therefore don't require constant care and compassion.

350 words

Original 417 words

18 marks

Examiner

- This essay is detailed.
- It uses a range of references and quotations.
- These are used to write about the poet's ideas.
- There are enough of these to give a developed interpretation of the poem.
- The focus on interpretations is the strongest feature of this essay.
- To get a higher mark in Level 5, the student should name specific techniques and link these to the poet's ideas.

Mr Salles Checklist of Essay Skills	
Thesis statement with one simple explanation	N
Thesis statement with two or more parts.	N
Form	N
Structure	Y
Quotes from the beginning	Y
Quotes from the middle	Y
Quotes from the end	N
Number of one word quotes analysed	3
Number of quotes whether analysed or not	11
Number of techniques	5
Number of exploratory words	0
Connectives to suggest alternative interpretation	0
Conclusion	Y

Mr Salles

So, this student, like all the students getting 18 marks so far, has not written about the ending. This is such an easy way to improve.

The comment about enjambment does link to the poet's ideas, so does count as structure, even though the examiner's report says don't bother with this technique!

But, there is also no thesis statement.

This essay is a valuable clue as to what other things make it so easy to get a grade 7:

Techniques, and **one word quotes.** They have to be linked to meanings and the poet's ideas. Then write a **conclusion**. It really is that simple.

Imagine if the student had also written about the ending, and linked it all together at the beginning with a thesis statement!

For Grade 7

Mr Salles Checklist of Essay Skills							
Response	15	16	17	18	19	20	Ave
Thesis statement with one simple explanation	N	N	N	N	N	N	N
Thesis statement with two or more parts.	Y	Y	Y	Y	Y	N	Y
Form	N	N	N	N	Y	N	N
Structure	Y	Y	Y	Y	Y	Y	Y
Quotes from the beginning	Y	Y	Y	Y	Y	Y	Y
Quotes from the middle	Y	Y	Y	Y	Y	Y	Y
Quotes from the end	Y	N	N	N	N	N	N
Number of one word quotes analysed	5	3	3	3	4	3	3
Number of quotes whether analysed or not	11	6	6	10	10	11	9
Number of techniques	4	3	3	7	12	5	6
Number of exploratory words	4	0	0	0	3	0	1
Connectives to suggest alternative interpretation	2	0	0	0	1	0	0
Conclusion	Y	N	N	Y	Y	Y	Y

This is a very surprising result. A grade 7 answer contains many of the same ingredients as a grade 6 answer.

The significant difference is that at grade 7, students tend to write a more thoughtful thesis statement.

Grade 6 Word Count		
Answer	Student	Me
Response 10	247	179
Response 11	262	195
Response 12	274	184
Response 13	277	196
Response 14	319	238
Grade 7 Word Count		
Average	**276**	**198**
Response 15	321	258
Response 16	419	287
Response 17	461	305
Response 18	340	300
Response 19	403	303
Response 20	417	350
Average	**394**	**300**

So, word count is the real difference. Students at grade 7 write more. They aren't making more points, using more quotes or writing about more techniques. They are simply writing about them in more detail – linking them to the poet's ideas.

A grade 7 student writes 33% more.

19 marks (Grade 8)

Response 21

Bold presents autumn as a season which changes the appearance of everything. The poem begins bluntly, **"Autumn sneaks in like a pick pocket"**. It suggests the change to the natural world will be negative. The IMAGE *may* be deliberately shocking and unexpected.

In addition, autumn is portrayed as altering nature's colours. The SIMILE **"like a pick pocket"** suggests that the annual appearance of autumn has honed a skill in being able to alter nature quickly, like a pick pocket practises their skill. The phrase **"pick pocket"** includes the idea of secrecy in this skill of changing the colours of trees and sky. This IMAGERY portrays autumn as full of life.

Furthermore, Bold adds to the IMAGE of autumn being a trouble maker, and a bringer of chaos. His **"windy sidekick"** **"misdirects by waving handkerchiefs of colour"**. This association with wind explains why autumn is easily dislikeable. This sense of chaos is an undesirable experience for people.

Moreover, autumn changes **"the once soothing horizon"** so that it **"rages with reddening cheeks"**. This implies that autumn has angered the earth in response to the poor weather it brings. **"Reddening cheeks"** also suggests that nature has been changed in undesirable ways. The PERSONIFICATION of nature also invites the reader to share the same human emotions.

The use of the adjective **"reddening"** hints at the idea that autumn also has a positive effect in bringing colour. This is emphasised by the **"waving handkerchiefs of colour"**. So, <u>*although*</u> autumn removes the shades of green and heat of summer, it brings with it a positive range of colours. This IMAGERY also sounds like an entertainer, which suggests that autumn can also be a season of joy and positivity.

282 words

Original 410 words

19 marks

Examiner

- This essay responds clearly to the question and to the poem
- By half way it starts to score Level 5 for AO2 and AO1
- Focusing on single word quotations means that the references are integrated into explanations.
- Techniques are also interpreted.
- All the interpretations are linked to the poet's ideas.
- This puts the essay at the top of Level 5.

Mr Salles Checklist of Essay Skills	
Thesis statement with one simple explanation	Y
Thesis statement with two or more parts.	N
Form	N
Structure	N
Quotes from the beginning	Y
Quotes from the middle	Y
Quotes from the end	Y
Number of one OR TWO word quotes analysed	3
Number of quotes whether analysed or not	10
Number of techniques	6
Number of exploratory words	1
Connectives to suggest alternative interpretation	1
Conclusion	N

Mr Salles

Writing about the ending of the poem, even without naming it as the ending, has allowed the student to show a full understanding of the poet's ideas.

Although the student hasn't written a proper conclusion, the last paragraph is about the ending, and about the poet's ideas. So the examiner has treated it as a conclusion.

Because the student has written about the beginning and the ending, and used these to explain the poet's ideas, the examiner is happy that the student has written about structure. Even though the student has mentioned nothing about structure at all!

Just write about "the human condition". Autumn has no meaning, and the outside world has no meaning, except in so far as humans experience it: "This IMAGERY also sounds like an entertainer, which suggests that autumn can also be a season of joy and positivity."

20 marks

Response 22
The poet uses a CONTRAST of a small boy next to dangerous traffic to explore ideas about how we should care for each other.

The father carries the boy as **"he cradles the earth's most fragile treasure"**, which hasn't been **"labelled"**. The idea of **"fragile treasure"** is linked to **"but it's unlabelled"** by ENJAMBMENT. This suggests that the important nature of the treasure is being kept secret. The run on line makes us read **"but it's unlabelled"** immediately after reading **"most fragile treasure"**. It suggests the treasure isn't being kept safe somewhere where it would be labelled, like a museum, but is out in the world where it can be damaged. **"But it's unlabelled"** makes us fearful that somewhere in the next three STANZAS the father and son will not be treated with care. **"Labelled"** reveals that none of us carry labels, we *may* be vulnerable, but others cannot know this. Consequently, we should treat everyone as **"precious treasure"**.

This message is emphasised by the cyclical STRUCTURE of the poem. The poem begins with **"road"** and **"rainfall"**, and ends with **"The cars will never stop rolling"** and **"The weather will never begin to care"**. **"The cars will never stop rolling"** REPRESENTS the many people we will encounter in our lives, with different histories. **"The weather will never begin to care"** suggests that the world will always introduce barriers, which we can only overcome with support from others. The REPETITION of **"never"** shows how the only solution is protecting each other. This father and son are a symbol of those in society who are vulnerable, easily exploited by the powerful who are REPRESENTED by the cars.

The poet uses the pronoun **"we"** to emphasise that we all share the responsibility of protecting others. The poet states **"This world won't let us live if we won't shoulder each other"**. The word **"shoulder"** emphasises the father's height and strength, allowing him to carry his son safely. Linking this to **"we"** shows that we must all protect others in the same way. He SYMBOLISES the strong protecting the vulnerable, so that we will all live.

This penultimate STANZA is not punctuated until the final full stop. This is a CONTRAST to the other STANZAS, and marks it out visually as important, as this is where the poet states their main viewpoint. The final line of this STANZA **"shoulder each other"** reflects this viewpoint, because it sounds like an instruction.

To conclude, Nye emphasises the importance of caring for and protecting each other at all times, as everyone is vulnerable at some time in their lives, and we can never know when or who needs help.

440 words

Original 492 words

20 marks

Examiner

- This is long enough to be considered detailed.
- It is developed because, even from the first sentence, it deals with the poet's message.
- This first sentence acts as a thesis statement.
- This is a brilliant way to begin, because it lets the examiner know that the essay is already "thoughtful" in Level 5.
- The range of references used in the explanations make this a "developed" essay.
- The range of poet's ideas explained also makes it "developed".
- The comments about the father and son being a symbol of society show that the student fully understands the extended METAPHOR in this poem.
- The essay deals with a range of named techniques, like SYMBOL, which are linked to the poet's ideas.
- So overall this is "considered" and "thoughtful".
- To get into Level 6, the student should write about one more technique in detail, linking it to the poet's ideas.

Mr Salles Checklist of Essay Skills	
Thesis statement with one simple explanation	Y
Thesis statement with two or more parts.	N
Form	N
Structure	Y
Quotes from the beginning	Y
Quotes from the middle	Y
Quotes from the end	Y
Number of one word quotes analysed	4
Number of quotes whether analysed or not	21
Number of techniques	9
Number of exploratory words	0
Connectives to suggest alternative interpretation	0
Conclusion	Y

Mr Salles

Thesis statement, conclusion, beginning and end. Including these is key to a grade 8.

The links to the poet's ideas are great. The examiner wants just one more thing – another technique or two.

But wait, aren't there 9 already? Yes, but look at how many of them are about structure! Everything except *represent* and *symbolise*.

70

The examiner couldn't care less about all the other aspects of structure. Repetition is more than enough.

They want the rest of the techniques to be poetic devices – but just the obvious ones. Simile, metaphor, personification, alliteration, sibilance. Any of those will keep them very happy indeed, *so long as you link what you find to the poet's ideas.*

Response 23

In this poem, Macrae explores her ideas about what it means to live a happy life. The poem uses frequent ENJAMBMENT to show how life is continuous and flowing, and that the key to living a happy life is to join that flow, rather than interrupt or fight it. At other times, END STOPPED lines suggest that, within that flow, life will throw up obstacles and complications. *However*, we are reassured that these can be overcome, and that life's flow will continue.

Macrae has also rejected a RHYME scheme. This conveys a further message that happiness does not need perfection, simply a positive outlook. The man in this poem REPRESENTS these ideas. Though he is **"aged"** and **"his face was furrowed by the wind and plough"**, his happiness is suggested by **"His eyes were filled with sunlight"**. This **"sunlight"** SYMBOLISES happiness which comes from within, rather than external factors.

Furthermore, his friends value him even after he has died, so at the funeral **"the congregation were baptised in their own tears"**. JUXTAPOSING the sadness of **"tears"** with being **"baptised"**, which we associate with hope and heaven, implies that Harry's life changed his friends for the better. They are closer to a heaven of happiness than before they met him. *Although* there is never any reference to Harry having a religious faith, the way he has lived a simple life without material wealth, is like the life of a holy man. He appears to have been happier than people who pursue **"wealth"** or a **"mansion"**.

Day to day he has only **"his working dogs"** and his **"flock"** of sheep, but he is happy *perhaps* because of the simplicity of his life. The PERSONIFICATION of **his "flock" "rolling down the mountain like a pregnant sky"** suggests that he brings happiness, like a new life, into the valley. The sheep *may* also be brought down from the mountain at winter, not just to avoid the cold, but because they too will be pregnant with lambs. This portrays Harry's nurturing of his flock, and REPRESENTS his kindness and generosity towards others.

In conclusion, his care for his **"flock"** illustrates that looking after them causes him to be happy. It also shows us that he has a positive impact on all living things. Macrae emphasises Harry's lack of possessions and comfort, and suggests that this *may* be a cause of his contentment, as he is **"happy in a cabin"** rather than a house.

408 words

Original 510 words

20 marks

Examiner

- This essay is long enough to be detailed and developed.
- It explains the poet's ideas from the very start.
- Paragraphs 1 and 2 are already "clear understanding" for level 4, because the explanations are clear
- And because the explanations refer to the poet's ideas.
- It also has a range of references and quotations.
- And a range of techniques to explain the poet's ideas.
- The essay becomes "thoughtful" in Level 5 when it analyses single word quotations, with "baptised", "wealth" and "mansion".
- These embedded quotations are used to explain the poet's ideas.
- The rest of the essay is all Level 5 quality of explanation.
- To get into Level 6, the student should explore a longer explanation of one or more techniques, showing how that reveals the poet's ideas about happiness.

Mr Salles Checklist of Essay Skills	
Thesis statement with one simple explanation	Y
Thesis statement with two or more parts.	N
Form	N
Structure	Y
Quotes from the beginning	Y
Quotes from the middle	Y
Quotes from the end	Y
Number of one word quotes analysed	3
Number of quotes whether analysed or not	14
Number of techniques	8
Number of exploratory words	2
Connectives to suggest alternative interpretation	2
Conclusion	Y

Mr Salles

Those first two paragraphs were packed with an analysis of structure. The examiner ignored it, awarding Level 4.

Structure kicks in at Level 5, so you can see these comments about structure have not scored at all.

This is proof that they actually don't care about structure, other than beginning and end.

In the examiner's defence, those two paragraphs make some pretty far fetched claims about the effect of structure, through enjambment and end stopped lines. It is why the examiners wish they had never put the criteria in the mark scheme. The student's comments are what they call, in the examiner's reports, "spurious". And I agree.

I can give credit to the comment about the rhyme scheme. But the examiner doesn't. The student deals with the beginning and the end and that is enough for them.

I love the comment about juxtaposition. The examiner will probably agree that this is a worthwhile comment about structure, but that the student doesn't need it to get the structure mark. They are quite happy to see it as a technique about language, with a great link to the poet's ideas.

As usual, there are a load of techniques, but the examiner just gets excited about the ones about language – the normal descriptive techniques: symbol, representation, personification.

Which one do they probably like best? Symbol.

They want another one.

For Grade 8

Response	21	22	23	Ave
Thesis statement with one simple explanation	Y	Y	Y	Y
Thesis statement with two or more parts.	N	N	N	N
Form	N	N	N	N
Structure	N	Y	Y	Y
Quotes from the beginning	Y	Y	Y	Y
Quotes from the middle	Y	Y	Y	Y
Quotes from the end	Y	Y	Y	Y
Number of one word quotes analysed	3	4	3	3
Number of quotes whether analysed or not	10	21	14	15
Number of techniques	6	9	8	8
Number of exploratory words	1	0	2	1
Connectives to suggest alternative interpretation	1	0	2	1
Conclusion	N	Y	Y	Y
Word total	410	492	510	471

We can see some dramatic changes once students achieve grade 8.

There is another big jump in the number of words students write. But these words are used to write about many more quotes – 15 instead of 9.

They identify many more techniques – 8 instead of 6 (6 was a high figure due to response 19 dramatically inflating the average).

The message is clear – if you can explain how the techniques reveal the poet's ideas, you will score marks.

The more of these explanations you write, the higher your mark will be.

Let's see if this pattern holds true at Grade 9.

21 marks (Grade 9)

Response 24

The poet portrays the city as dark and foreboding at night-time. Our first impressions are neutral. The city has **"black cabs which trundle"** and **"men about town who strut the pavements"**. But a closer inspection reveals the **"stare"** of the **"harsh, street lights"**. These lights are portrayed as sinister, as the poet suggests London has a deceptive night-time appearance. People *appear* to bring corruption to the city streets.

Lowell uses a sinister, gothic SEMANTIC FIELD, with **"harsh"**, **"dirty and dangerous"**, **"caged"** and **"pulses"**. The ALLITERATION of **"dirty and dangerous"** emphasises a sense of threat, and suggests that the visual attractiveness of the city at night hides a dangerous reality. Lovell portrays the corrupt power of the city by CONTRASTING it with the moon: **"the city has eclipsed her light"**. This REPRESENTS how nature cannot bring literal light, or the SYMBOLIC light of truth, to the city. This *could* be a criticism of modern society and electric light pollution, which **"blisters icily"**, causing such damage that even nature can find no cure for our actions.

The absence of a RHYME scheme *might* direct us to this message. London is one of the wealthiest and largest cities in the world, and the lack of RHYME creates a disappointed TONE which reflects the poet's view of the city and the damage it causes to the natural world.

This TONE of disappointment is also reflected in the poet's choice of title, focusing on **"2 A.M."** This highlights how, though most citizens are fast asleep, the city continues with its damaging actions.

In conclusion, the poem *could* act as a warning that, when its readers awake, the damage to the environment and by extension to the wider world, will already have occurred while they slept.

290 words

Original 390 words

21 marks

Examiner

- The mention of "foreboding" in Paragraph 1 immediately shows the student has a developed understanding.
- The first sentence therefore acts as a thesis statement.
- References and quotations are always linked to an interpretation of the poet's ideas.
- By the end of Paragraph 2, the essay's argument begins to be "convincing" rather than "thoughtful".
- This convincing argument is maintained till the end of the essay, which means it achieves Level 6 for AO1.
- The interpretation of "dirty and dangerous" is thoughtful, so achieves Level 5 AO2. This is because it is linked to the interpretation of the poet's ideas.
- However, the comments on the lack of a RHYME scheme aren't well explained and don't link well to an interpretation. This is an area of development to get a higher mark in Level 6.
- Overall, this is an exploratory essay, and moves in to Level 6.

Mr Salles Checklist of Essay Skills	
Thesis statement with one simple explanation	N
Thesis statement with two or more parts.	Y
Form	N
Structure	Y
Quotes from the beginning	Y
Quotes from the middle	Y
Quotes from the end	N
Number of one or two word quotes analysed	1
Number of quotes whether analysed or not	13
Number of techniques	8
Number of exploratory words	3
Connectives to suggest alternative interpretation	0
Conclusion	Y

Mr Salles

This is interesting. The examiner says, "there is no quote from the end, so there is no comment about structure". The examiner says, "the stuff about rhyme is spurious, and is therefore not a comment about structure".

So, how does it get into Level 6? Contrast. Contrast is a structural technique.

The marking criteria says you need to write about "form" in Level 6. That's why the student wrote about the absence of a rhyme scheme. But no, it appears that this is a zombie part of the mark scheme (it is either dead, fictitious, or eats itself).

There is no form. Apparently, a poem is just a collection of words about "the human condition".

Paragraph 2 has persuaded the examiner this is a top answer. Very few students identify a semantic field, and even fewer manage to link that to the poet's ideas. There are 5 techniques and 6 quotes, all linked together.

Notice how the examiner has not mentioned the word 'exploratory' before. The student has easily shown they are being exploratory by using 3 of those words: could, appear, might.

PEE Sentences

Look again at paragraph 2.

The first 2 sentences are PEE sentences. They each contain a Point, some Evidence and an Explanation. They also both name a technique.

"Lowell uses a sinister, gothic SEMANTIC FIELD, with **"harsh", "dirty and dangerous", "caged"** and **"pulses"**."

Notice that PEE doesn't have to appear in order. The point is the use of a gothic semantic field. The explanation is that this makes the words sound 'sinister'. The evidence is not one quote, but four!

"The ALLITERATION of **"dirty and dangerous"** emphasises a sense of threat, and suggests that the visual attractiveness of the city at night hides a dangerous reality."

Here PEE is in that order. The point is that the writer uses alliteration. Then the single quote is the evidence. But, there are two explanations. The first is about the sense of threat, the second is about how this is more threatening, because this is hidden and disguised.

That's how you get top grades.

PEE sentences, not paragraphs.

22 marks

Response 25

Nye explores ideas about the necessity for all of us to protect and take care for each other. She suggests that life will always be full of challenges for everyone, so we will all need protection. The final lines, **"The cars will never stop rolling / The weather will never begin to care"** implies that the world will always be a threat, so we will have to maintain a sense of care. The ANAPHORA of this couplet emphasises this message, as does the END STOPPING of each line. This sums up the poem's message.

The father in this poem, and his treatment of his son, SYMBOLISES the necessity of our care for each other. The only other COUPLET also uses ANAPHORA, in this case **"No wheel"** and **"No spray"**. This, and the brevity of the lines, emphasise how much care the father takes of his son.

The verb **"dare"** in **"No splash dare soak him"** conveys the father's determination. That **"No wheel dare shadow his steps"** also emphasises this, especially as the idea of a car following the father's footstep is slightly ridiculous.

The poet also chooses ASSERTIVE VOCABULARY, to insist on her message. She states **"This world won't let us live / If we won't shoulder each other"**. The REPETITION of **"won't"** conveys her certainty that we must look after each other.

In conclusion, the father's treatment of his son is therefore a SYMBOL, instructing us to treat all others with care and kindness.

245 words

Original 325 words

22 marks

Examiner

- The first two sentences are a detailed thesis statement.
- These show the student has engaged with the poet's ideas at a high level.
- The student regularly comments on named techniques, linking them to explanations of the poet's ideas.
- Towards the end of the poem, there are enough of these to be analytical.
- The discussion of TONE is a very analytical explanation of a technique, linked to the poet's ideas.
- The student has cleverly written about the poet's point of view at the beginning and end of the poem. This shows that they have dealt with the whole task, even though the essay is short.
- However, to get a higher mark, the student would need to write some detailed explanations about some other moments in the poem.

Mr Salles Checklist of Essay Skills	
Thesis statement with one simple explanation	N
Thesis statement with two or more parts.	Y
Form	N
Structure	Y
Quotes from the beginning	Y
Quotes from the middle	Y
Quotes from the end	Y
Number of one and two word quotes analysed	4
Number of quotes whether analysed or not	8
Number of techniques	8
Number of exploratory words	0
Connectives to suggest alternative interpretation	0
Conclusion	Y

Mr Salles

There is that pattern again.

- Write about the beginning and ending.
- Have a thesis and a conclusion.
- Use short quotes and link everything to the poet's ideas.

Repetition is always a structural technique which the examiner likes, because it is always easy to link this to the poet's ideas. Anaphora is just a particular kind of repetition, so the examiner is very happy.

The comment about end-stopped lines probably counts for nothing. So too that another quote is a couplet. This is because they aren't linked to the poet's ideas.

Did you notice that this student wrote about the end of the poem straight after the thesis statement? This is definitely a useful technique if you want to use it. It makes writing about the beginning a little trickier – for me it is just easier to write about the beginning first, and then write about the ending with the conclusion. But, you don't have to do it my way.

Notice how the conclusion comes back to the poet's wider point or, in the words of the touchy feely examiner, "the human condition". Notice too that the conclusion includes the magic word: 'symbol'.

To get higher marks the student needs to write about other moments in the poem – in other words, the middle! Maybe they ran out of time? Maybe they forgot, because they started with the ending.

24 marks

Response 26
Lowell's speaker embraces the beauty of night-time in the city. <u>However</u>, she expresses her simultaneous disgust at the corrupt society exposed by the** "pale and pallid" **moon.

Throughout the poem, she uses ENJAMBMENT to add a political viewpoint to her apparently neutral description of life in the city. The fourth line ends on the verb **"spills"**, which invites us to think about the connotation of waste or *perhaps* bloodshed. This leads to how Lowell presents the city as deceptive and dangerous, JUXTAPOSING **"men about town"** with **"vagabonds"** who sleep in a **"stupor"** in the city's **"harsh"** streets. This IMAGERY offers a critical perspective on the divisions of social class in society.

This social division is also reflected in the segregation evident in the description of London's cabs, **"black cabs trundle, / First one, / A second follows"**. The speaker appears disgusted at this division as **"dirty and dangerous"**, so that the city feels like **"a foreign country"**. This **"foreign"** nature of the city emphasises that this division doesn't feel natural. The oppressive character of the city is also portrayed with the REPETITION of **"caged"** to imply that the streetlights create a SYMBOLIC cage of dark and light stripes on the streets.

The cruelty of this lighting is also reflected in the **"stare"** of the **"harsh, street lights"**. They also SYMBOLISE the harshness the speaker believes has become typical of how those in London society treat each other. This is CONTRASTED with the speaker's love of the moon, **"she is my sister"**. This PERSONIFICATION implies the moon has human values which are in direct CONTRAST with those of people in the city. Because the moon is timeless, we are invited to see that the modern **"city"** would be better if it incorporated the moral values of more ancient societies. She implies that new technology and better infrastructure shouldn't rob us of our morality or compassion.

The speaker *may* also criticise the spread of consumerism in the city. So the moon's **"light"** SYMBOLISES our moral values, which have no effect on the city, because its inhabitants are obsessed with all that is shiny and glittery, which the poet describes as **"blisters"**, suggesting that it is morally corrupt. The CONTRAST of **"blisters"** with **"icily"** also implies that the citizens are damaged by their materialism.

Personifying the moon as a **"sister"** REPRESENTS nature as having human values <u>in contrast</u> to their absence in the city below. This is why the city has become **"a foreign country"**, and why she loves the moon, even though it is **"pale and pallid"**. The TONE used to describe the moon in this STANZA is less harsh than the TONE of the STANZAS describing the city.

The poet chooses more harmonious sounds to emphasise her preference for the moon and the natural world. She loves the moon as **"my sister"**, <u>in contrast</u> to the **"dirty and dangerous"** city. This implies that she wants us to reject urban living and seek a more pastoral life in nature, so that we can reconnect with our moral values.

In conclusion, we *might* see the poem as a direct appeal to ask us to reject city life entirely. She portrays the city at night rather than day because this is when the CONTRAST between the natural world and the **"dirty and dangerous"** man-made city is most visible. Night also exposes social inequality. This setting allows Lowell to bring the SYMBOLIC **"light"** of nature and morality as a CONTRAST to the corrupt city.

580 words

Original 715 words

24 marks

Examiner

- The essay begins with a detailed thesis statement.
- This immediately suggests that the essay will be conceptualised.
- The second sentence tells us that the essay will argue for more than one perspective, which also makes it conceptualised.
- The student uses a high level of vocabulary, which allows them to be precise.
- The student names a variety of techniques.
- The explanations of these techniques is always linked to the poet's ideas.
- The whole essay is structured as an argument that proves the thesis.

Mr Salles Checklist of Essay Skills	
Thesis statement with one simple explanation	N
Thesis statement with two or more parts.	Y
Form	N
Structure	Y
Quotes from the beginning	Y
Quotes from the middle	Y
Quotes from the end	Y
Number of one and two word quotes analysed	9
Number of quotes whether analysed or not	25
Number of techniques	16
Number of exploratory words	2
Connectives to suggest alternative interpretation	2
Conclusion	Y

Mr Salles

You have about 35 minutes for this question. This student wrote 715 words. That is not many, if you work it out by the minute.

It is only 21 words per minute.

But, without handwriting practice, most students simply won't do this. Only grade 9 students seem to practise handwriting speed.

So, this answer has everything in the mark scheme but form, and yet scores 100%. Form is obviously not required.

You don't have to be as brilliant at writing as this student. Let's look at the basics of how it scores marks.

- It has the best thesis statement we have seen, with more than one idea. And the ideas are juxtaposed – the student says, pay attention, because I am going to show you a deeper meaning.

- The student knows that contrast will be a key technique in every single poem they ever read. So, they go looking for it.

- They know that symbolism will be a key technique in every single poem they ever read. So they look for that too.

- They (incorrectly, as it turns out) believe that they have to write about structure, so they ask themselves, what structural technique will be in nearly every poem I read? Enjambment. So they go looking for that.

- They (also incorrectly, as it turns out) believe that they need to write about form, so they go looking for stanzas. Every poem has at least one!

- They needn't have bothered. As you know by now, beginning and ending are enough form and structure.

- Repetition, contrast and juxtaposition are also structural techniques. But, the examiner is happy to treat them as language techniques, and you get the credit for them there.

Of course, every technique is linked to the poet's purpose. Many students have realised that if you simply write about the tone of the poem, you are always writing about the poet's point of view in a sophisticated way.

Response 27

Nye presents the necessity of care for others, and for protection of the vulnerable. These responsibilities are closely associated with the idea of love. Nye uses ASSERTIVE LANGUAGE to reveal how society can only function if we protect others.

"No splash dare soak him" creates an urgent TONE, and portrays the absolute importance of protection and care. Nye hopes to persuade the reader to share this belief in helping others in order to improve society. This IMAGERY also portrays the father as a hero in a battle with urban life, in order to show the act of protection as an example of bravery in the face of dangerous **"wheel"s,** or **"weather"**. The lines toward the end **"This world won't let us live/ if we won't shoulder each other"** emphasises the need to protect the vulnerable.

Nye also uses ENJAMBMENT to convey this message. The ENJAMBMENT introducing **"if we won't shoulder each other"** emphasises how we can't just choose to protect and care for others at particular moment, it must be a constant way of treating others. There is no regular line pattern to the STANZAS. This reflects the unpredictability of life's challenges, and the need to therefore be ready to care for others. This is treated as a loving act, because it is done unconditionally, without knowing in advance what future challenges will arise. So it is a lifelong commitment and responsibility.

The father is portrayed as knowing this is a lifelong responsibility, SYMBOLISED in the final line **"The weather will never begin to care."** The weather is an extended METAPHOR in the poem, REPRESENTING the many difficulties the father will face in looking after his son's welfare. This makes us reflect on how we should protect others, and of the long term nature of this responsibility. This presents the duty of caring for others as a long term burden.

To conclude, Nye suggests that society can only function fully if we all take on the responsibilities of caring for others, especially those who are vulnerable.

336 words

Original 650 words

24 marks

Examiner

- The first three sentences are a thesis statement which show at least a thoughtful, and *perhaps* exploratory understanding of the poet's ideas.
- The student refers to several specific moments in the poem, to show a range of references.
- These are all used to explain the poet's ideas about social responsibility.
- A strong explanation of these can be seen in the analysis of the effects of ENJAMBMENT.
- The most impressive analysis is of the extended METAPHOR about the weather.
- It is always linked to the poet's ideas.
- The range of references is always precisely chosen to help explain these ideas.
- So, overall this is exploratory and convincing.

Mr Salles Checklist of Essay Skills	
Thesis statement with one simple explanation	N
Thesis statement with two or more parts.	Y
Form	N
Structure	Y
Quotes from the beginning	Y
Quotes from the middle	N
Quotes from the end	Y
Number of one word quotes analysed	0
Number of quotes whether analysed or not	6
Number of techniques	10
Number of exploratory words	0
Connectives to suggest alternative interpretation	0
Conclusion	Y

Mr Salles

Writing about society is always a sophisticated way of writing about the poet's ideas.

The examiner has ignored the student's comments about enjambment and stanzas as explanations of structure. They have focused on how the explanation about enjambment leads to explaining the poet's ideas.

The examiner ignores the structure paragraph – the comments on stanzas, because the student writes about the ending. This is enough of a focus on the poem's structure.

Response 28

Angelou creates a speaker who views aging as a natural process. She criticises the "pity" and "tears" of the young, highlighting how life for the old is still worthwhile.

There is an irregular RHYME scheme, but in places Angelou uses ABCB. This *might* SYMBOLISE a natural cycle, similar to aging, which is simply a part of life, rather than a cause of grief. She uses IMPERATIVES and EXCLAMATION MARKS to instruct the reader, **"Stop! Hold your tears! Wait! Hold your pity!"** The speaker asserts their independence by refusing **"pity"**. The EXCLAMATION MARKS imply that the speaker *may* be shouting, which inverts the idea that the old are hard of hearing. She suggests instead that it is the young who won't listen and see the stereotype of aging, rather than listening to their elders. The speaker feels forced to be assertive as the young seek to make decisions for them.

The REPETITION of **"missing some"** at the end of the poem is JUXTAPOSED with the final line, which is positive. The negative TONE of **"missing some"** *perhaps* reflects the view of the young toward old age, and implies the idea of loss, that the old are therefore less than whole, and so are inferior and helpless. *However*, the CONTRAST with **"blessed"** shows that the speaker feels they are more complete than most. It implies that plenty of her peers have not been so **"blessed"**, and have died. The speaker's survival should instead be seen as a mark of their resilience and ability.

24 marks – I checked

251 words

Original 246 words

Examiner

- This student shows the virtue of being concise, saying as much as possible with as few words as possible.
- The thesis statement is conceptualised from the beginning, because it links the poet's ideas to quotations straight away.
- The quotations are embedded, so they are integrated into the explanation.
- They choose precise references to explain the poet's ideas.
- The student names the techniques the poet uses and links these to the poet's ideas.
- The essay deals with the whole of the text, beginning, middle and end.

Mr Salles Checklist of Essay Skills	
Thesis statement with one simple explanation	N
Thesis statement with two or more parts.	Y
Form	Y
Structure	Y
Quotes from the beginning	Y
Quotes from the middle	Y
Quotes from the end	Y
Number of one word quotes analysed	3
Number of quotes whether analysed or not	9
Number of techniques	10
Number of exploratory words	3
Connectives to suggest alternative interpretation	1
Conclusion	N

Mr Salles

We know that to gain marks for structure you must write about the beginning and ending, which this student does.

The comments about punctuation are also structural points linked to the poet's ideas, so this works. Repetition and juxtaposition are also structural techniques, and these are very well linked to explain the poet's ideas.

I would never give this 24/24. It doesn't even have a conclusion. (Although you could treat the last sentence as a conclusion).

I think the comment about the rhyme scheme is rubbish or 'spurious'. And it deals with hardly any quotations.

But, I am delighted that I am wrong. It proves that what gets the marks is:

Thesis statement, writing about the beginning and ending, the poet's tone, contrast and repetition.

In order to make this count, you have to write about the poet's ideas.

The ideas that the examiners like are those about "the human condition" – in this case, the attitude of the young towards old age; the attitude of the old to those who are young; their attitude to their own aging and survival.

The "human condition" is explored by seeking out the "timeless truths" – those things about being human which have always been, and will always be true.

When you read it back with this in mind, you'll see that "the human condition" is everywhere in this answer.

Response 29

Bold portrays the effect of autumn as destructive and undesirable. We can see autumn is destructive through the SEMANTIC FIELD Bold chooses, **"rattle"**, **"smacked"**, **"smothering"** and **"rages"**. The word **"smothering"** portrays autumn as oppressing nature, emphasising the enormous impact autumn brings. Bold STRUCTURES the poem with FREE VERSE and ENJAMBMENT, which emphasise the disruption of order and control caused by autumn. The impact is so powerful, that lines feel forced to overflow to the next line.

Autumn is also PERSONIFIED as a **"pick pocket"** and **"partner in crime"** to suggest that autumn's disruptive acts are deliberate and criminally evil. <u>Despite</u> this, Bold also portrays autumn as a positive season. The SIMILE **"like a pick pocket"** suggests that we can prepare, knowing autumn's characteristics.

"Autumn sneaks in" which also implies that autumn has to be so secretive because people are already prepared for its arrival. Bold portrays autumn as bringing joyful colours to the landscape, **"waving handkerchiefs of colour"**. **"Waving"** also connotes joy, and so we can view autumn as a positive force. In the final line, Bold JUXTAPOSES **"Rages with reddening cheeks"** to the **"once soothing horizon"**. <u>Although</u> **"Rages"** suggests anger, the fact that it is only in the **"cheeks"** suggests it is not dangerous. Moreover, the ALLITERATION with **"reddening"** also emphasises the changing beauty of nature as the sky is also filled with colour.

225 words

Original 245 words

24 marks

Examiner

- This is what a precise and concise essay looks like.
- It chooses specific vocabulary – the right words can be used to say more with fewer words.
- Every sentence explains an analysis of language, or techniques.
- All these explanations are linked to the poet's idea.
- Some sentences include quotation, analysis and explanation of language, technique and the poet's idea in the same sentence, rather than spending a whole paragraph to do it.
- The essay starts with a thesis statement with an overview of the poet's ideas.
- The student picks precise quotations, many of them single words, and links them to the poet's ideas.
- The student writes about a large number of named techniques, and links these to the poet's ideas.

Mr Salles Checklist of Essay Skills	
Thesis statement with one simple explanation	N
Thesis statement with two or more parts.	Y
Form	Y
Structure	Y
Quotes from the beginning	Y
Quotes from the middle	Y
Quotes from the end	Y
Number of one word quotes analysed	6
Number of quotes whether analysed or not	16
Number of techniques	8
Number of exploratory words	0
Connectives to suggest alternative interpretation	2
Conclusion	N

Mr Salles

There is no actual conclusion, but the examiner sees that the whole of the last paragraph is about the ending of the poem, so they treat this as a conclusion.

The student has swamped even this short answer with lots of quotes, especially zooming in on particular words.

You know by now that the examiners love a semantic field.

A rhyme scheme is ordered, and free verse disrupts this. The comment linking this to the disruptive nature of autumn in the poem therefore works brilliantly. This is exactly how to write about form. Don't force it. There has to be an actual link you would be happy to defend.

I always recommend thinking about alternative interpretations, and to do that, recommend you simply using connectives like 'although' and 'however'. This student has done that.

Other students have done that in the thesis statement. See response 28 and 26 for example.

I also recommend a heap of techniques, one of which will always be 'contrast' or 'juxtaposition'.

Students who are good at literature will also be skilled at spotting a semantic field, metaphor, simile and personification. They then explain how these reveal the poet's ideas.

So, I can get behind this as a full mark answer.

For Grade 9

Mr Salles Checklist of Essay Skills							
Response	24	25	26	27	28	29	Ave
Thesis statement with one simple explanation	N	N	N	N	N	N	N
Thesis statement with two or more parts.	Y	Y	Y	Y	Y	Y	Y
Form	N	N	N	N	Y	Y	N
Structure	Y	Y	Y	Y	Y	Y	Y
Quotes from the beginning	Y	Y	Y	Y	Y	Y	Y
Quotes from the middle	Y	Y	Y	N	Y	Y	Y
Quotes from the end	N	Y	Y	Y	Y	Y	Y
Number of one word quotes analysed	1	4	9	0	3	6	4
Number of quotes whether analysed or not	13	8	25	6	9	16	13
Number of techniques	8	8	16	10	10	8	10
Number of exploratory words	3	0	2	0	3	0	1
Connectives to suggest alternative interpretation	0	0	2	0	1	2	1
Conclusion	Y	Y	Y	Y	N	N	Y
Words	410	325	715	650	246	245	432

Here it is the increase in quality of the thesis and the number of techniques which makes the difference to grade 9.

The word count is very diverse. It tells us that grade 9 can be achieved in two ways:

1. Through sheer hard work. In other words, do what grade 8 students do, but write more of it.

2. Or, learn to make just as many explanations about techniques and the poet's purpose with far fewer words.

The average of 432 is actually lower than the 471 written by grade 8 students!

In all the guides I have written, this is the only literature or language question where grade 9 students don't write more than grade 8 students.

I think this is because they are writing about an *unseen* poem – they haven't revised lots of knowledge and content that they have prepared in advance. There is therefore much less to say.

So, getting their ideas down is easier. Once they have written about beginning, middle and end, included a thesis statement, and a conclusion, they are done. (So long as they are all linked to you know what0.

The poet's ideas.

Printed in Great Britain
by Amazon